WAKE-UP CALL

WHAT EVERY ENTREPRENEURIAL LEADER NEEDS TO KNOW

WAKE-UP CALL

THE 7 PIVOTAL MOMENTS THAT CHANGE EVERYTHING

GLENN GUTEK

OVIEDO, FLORIDA, U.S.A.

Paperback ISBN: 978-1-939183-54-5
Hardback ISBN: 978-1-939183-67-5
Ebook ISBN: 978-1-939183-55-2
Published by HigherLife Publishing and Marketing, Inc.

400 Fontana Circle
Building 1, Suite 105
Oviedo, FL 32765
www.ahigherlife.com

Cover Design: Dimitreus Castro

First Edition

14 15 16 17 18 19 — 9 8 7 6 5 4 3 2 1
Printed in the United States of America

✑ TABLE OF CONTENTS ✑

✑ FOREWORD ✑

OVER THE YEARS, as a past dean and presently a professor of management in the Rollins College MBA program, I've had the honor of working with entrepreneurs in many different capacities. I've written about, trained, and consulted with them in starting and operating their businesses. I've helped them to develop and maintain strategic plans to help ensure success. I've also been personally involved in starting three different, presently ongoing, entrepreneurial ventures in three different industries.

My entrepreneurial experience tells me that Glenn Gutek's new book, *Wake-Up Call*, contains practical advice that every entrepreneur should take to heart. The book is overflowing with profound entrepreneurial insights written in clear, everyday language. As a bonus, one will find that reading the book is enjoyable because of the many practical examples. The insights discussed are pragmatic because they've grown out of the author's experience as an entrepreneurial consultant.

Gutek organizes his insights about entrepreneurship around the seven critical "wake-up calls"—seven trials and tribulations that all entrepreneurs face. These insights revolve around critical entrepreneurial topics like success, failure, change, and faith. The book alerts entrepreneurs to the invaluable conclusion that it's how one interprets and responds to these trials that determines how successful they will be.

Is there a better way to help entrepreneurs become successful than by listening to one that has helped others identify and solve problems in their own companies? I can't think of one. If you're an entrepreneur, do yourself a favor and read this book. Insights to help you become more successful are only a few pages away!

—Samuel C. Certo, PhD
Steinmetz Professor of Management
Crummer Graduate School of Business
Rollins College
Winter Park, Florida

∽ INTRODUCTION ∽

Take a few moments to examine the image above. What do you see? Think quietly about the possible interpretations. Do you see a bat? A mask of some sort? Some sort of fierce wolf-like creature? Here is a bit of a harder question that requires another step to answer: Do you see what you think others would see? Can you anticipate what other readings of the same visual might be?

This image is the first of ten traditionally used in the famous Rorschach test, also called the inkblot test. Most of us have seen these images before. The process that goes into this "test" is extremely sophisticated. Although it was invented in the 1920s, psychologists still use it widely. To the careful eye of the knowledgeable analyst, the test yields data about cognition and personality and illustrates response tendencies, personal and interpersonal styles, and more. Analysts pay attention to how long it takes for a respondent to start speaking, whether she focuses on the ink or white spaces in the ink, how much she stresses the symmetry of the blot, and into what major category of response her interpretation falls (e.g., animal, nature, human.)

Why is a book about the "wake-up calls of entrepreneurial leadership" starting with an explanation of some old psychological test? Rorschach's test works as a metaphor for this book in so many ways, but I'll start with the most basic. We live most of our lives trying to reduce the facts of the world to black and white. There are "good" and "bad" characters. There are the "right" and "wrong" religious, political, and philosophical belief systems. Events in our lives are opportunities for "joy" or "grief."

This book is based on the premise that most of life isn't black and white. There is certainly a time for clear and decisive action. But we should not allow a preference for simplicity to negate complexity. Most of the things that happen to us aren't good or bad. Even the worst of events can provide wonderful growth opportunities. Even the most fortuitous of events can result in terrible consequences. Given these facts, how we read those events and respond to them matters a great deal, both personally and certainly as leaders in our businesses. This book is an homage to gray. A few years ago, as I was driving around, I'd see a bumper sticker on numerous cars that said, "&$% happens." It is a simple and crudely explained statement, but altogether true. Things in life change. We encounter a variety of events we could hardly anticipate, and we do so regularly. What do you do when "stuff" happens to you?

This book argues that when stuff happens, there is a good chance that you can mitigate the negative results with the right perspective and approach. There is a good chance that you can turn the negatives, or the surprising events in your life, into positives with the right perspective. This book looks at common events as you would a daily Rorschach test. How you interpret them, and the actions that come out of them, says more about you than it says about the events. Our response to the things that happen to us makes us who we are. This book offers some strategies and frameworks for considering things that might just help us emerge from situations better than before.

Biography as Explanation

This book grew out of my personal experiences as a consultant. My company, Awake Consulting, works with attorneys, CPAs, insurance agents, general contractors, franchise owners, and other professionals. Many leaders want to take the next step in their careers. Often they are executives who want to become entrepreneurs. Sometimes they are middle managers who want to become high-level managers. Almost always, they approach us looking for answers to the question: *What do I need to do next?*

As a means of addressing that central question, first let me tell you a bit about the categorization of events you'll find in this book. Wake-up calls can come in so many different forms. They can be tragic and sudden. They can come in the form of terrible loss and tremendous gain. They can sneak up on you quietly and slowly, so that you don't even notice that something major has happened to your universe. They can come from both material and emotional sources, and usually *the only thing predictable about them is that they will happen eventually.*

The stories of every individual entrepreneur are unique. Every one of us faces our own hurdles, leverages our own strengths in unique ways, and comes to find our own version of success in different ways. But when you step back and think of the life of an entrepreneur broadly, certain themes emerge. The diagram below depicts how wake-up calls can alter our interpretation of events in our lives.

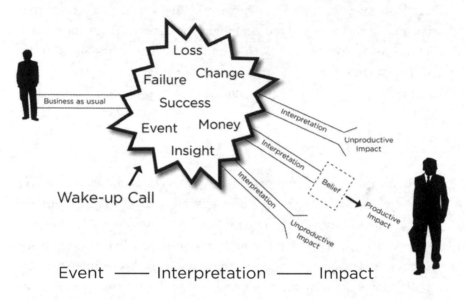

This particular journey is applicable to many of us, although it plays out in different ways depending on a person's unique situation. Through many years of working with hundreds of entrepreneurial leaders, and seeing common themes in their varying situations, I devised the seven "types" of wake-up calls. We all endure trials and tribulations. How we interpret these wake-up calls—and to what extent we use their lessons to move forward—is a defining aspect that determines whether we will derive long-term effectiveness from the experience or, instead, crash and burn. In the chapters to come, you'll read about these seven types of wake-up calls:

1. Insight

2. Success

3. Money

4. Failure

5. Loss

6. Change

7. Belief

Exactly what those headings mean will become clear. Suffice it to say, this book should apply to everyone, to varying degrees. We might not all have *every* one of those wake-up calls, but *every* one of us will have some. I've often heard the quote, when something totally unsurprising happens, that "there is nothing new under the sun." In my work with entrepreneurs, I've noticed a couple of common themes. Many times, these individuals are struggling to snap out of an old rut or to adjust to a new market reality. Other times, they are struggling to take the next big step after enjoying some initial success. Almost always, their difficulties have less to do with the events that surround them at work or home than with their interpretation of those problems. This book aims to compare the various ways in which people interpret and respond to common events. Can we approach the same sorts of problems in wildly unique ways, and with similarly different results? Aren't some approaches to problems much better in particular settings than others? Can we be more productive in our interpretations?

WHAT IS PRODUCTIVE INTERPRETATION?

What do I mean by interpreting in a productive way? One way to judge whether an event has been interpreted productively is to ask a simple question: *Does my reaction to this event take me to a better place? Does it sustain my passion and original vision or diminish it?* Another rule of thumb I use when thinking about interpretations is: *Does it broaden my perspective or narrow it? Does this help me grow or not?* I believe that our views in life should always be open to reexamination and, if necessary, change. Our perspectives about events should lead to a broadening perspective of life itself.

An age-old entrepreneurial story gets me to my final explanation of productive interpretation. We all know—anecdotally as well as personally—that two of every three business start-ups fail. There are a host of reasons for this. Maybe the premise for the start-up was a bad idea. Maybe the founders tried to operate a bad model. Perhaps they were underfunded or the timing was wrong. Regardless, I'm interested in what happens after the tents fold up. What does that failure mean? A very small percentage of entrepreneurs interpret those events in ways that motivate future success.

When I was fifteen, my dad left corporate America to buy a lumber yard and home-improvement center. The year was 1981, and interest rates soared to 18 percent, construction shut down and home improvement was not even a sitcom. After one year, the business shut down due to cash-flow issues and a poorly negotiated lease-purchase, and my dad returned to a corporate job. By 1984, Flagler County, the location of his failed home-improvement store and lumber yard, went on an unprecedented growth stretch that lasted until 2008. Rather than interpreting this experience as bad timing or a lesson learned, my dad opted to never venture into the world of entrepreneurship. When the opportunity came for his son to start a business, my dad hit the panic button and passionately discouraged such a risk. My dad's effort to frantically wave a cautionary flag did not stop me; I chose to employ aggressive marketing with being fiscally conservative as a strategy to bootstrap the business and not fail due to cash flow and marketplace challenges.

The final thing I'd say about productive interpretation is that, sooner or later, it is going to show up in sustainable, bottom-line results. Ha! Got you, didn't I? You picked this book up because you are a businessperson or entrepreneur. And you were wondering when I might get to that all-important business maxim. This sort of approach, whereby you work to interpret facts more productively, will actually manifest over the long term in increased revenues, better profitability, and more sustainable market share.

Even when you are that entrepreneur who failed at an initial effort, you can interpret your events in a way that leads to productive impact. Or you can give up and go home. Which do you choose? Come with me as we explore some helpful ways to respond productively. We will look at modern movies and public figures, famous examples of particular phenomena, sports, and politics—all as fertile soil in our attempts to glean some lessons. In so doing, you may wake up to your ultimate potential. You may improve and develop leadership skills. You may maximize your business results and gain that ever-important competitive advantage in the marketplace.

CHAPTER 1

AH-HA!
THE WAKE-UP CALL
OF INSIGHT

"Think left and think right and think low and think high.
Oh, the thinks you can think up if only you try!"
—DR. SEUSS

A s I MENTIONED in the introduction, there are many types of wake-up calls. Some will make more immediate sense to you, while some will feel a bit less counterintuitive. To help us get some momentum, and to start you out easy, I want to begin with one of the more basic "wake-up" calls. I also want to start with wake-up calls of the positive sort. After I introduce you to the more positive examples, we will progress to some of the more painful ones.

The thing to remember, though—and we will get to this in the conclusion of this book—is that your response to the painful and the positive wake-up calls will be, in many ways, the same. In both instances, you will be charged in a positive way to turn the page. Whether you are coming off the thrill of a high or the agony of a defeat, you still need to work to interpret those events in a way that will help you move forward.

LEARNING TO SPEAK MEANS CONTINUING
TO SPEAK

There is a great scene in *My Fair Lady* that now makes its way into montages of the best film moments in history. In broad strokes, the movie depicts the worldly and wealthy Professor Higgins, who bets a friend that he can turn an attractive Cockney woman named Eliza Doolittle—a bit rough around the edges at the onset of the film— into a truly refined "lady." One of the more well-known scenes finds this professor trying to teach Eliza, played by the inimitable Audrey Hepburn, how to pronounce words in a way that won't divulge her social status. "The *rine* in *spine*," as she pronounces it, must become "The *rain* in *Spain*." She must train her ears to the difference and then use that training. When she finally learns, Professor Higgins shouts enthusiastically, "By George, she's got it!"

Eliza has worked diligently on her pronunciation. She has practiced and struggled before finally experiencing success. This "awakening" came through effort and work. One of my favorite people in the world is a client from Massachusetts. I'll tell her story a bit later, but her phrase is one of those "ah-ha!" types. She is known to say, "I had a blinding flash of the obvious!" Sometimes, these moments seem obvious to us after the fact. Sometimes, we have been working on those moments in our own head, like Eliza and her "rain in Spain," for quite a while. We've been ruminating on things until finally, things suddenly grow crystalline and actionable. When the awakening does finally happen, it feels wonderful!

Other times, those sorts of moments appear all on their own, with no invitation. We don't work to bring them into being. We don't struggle with any great problem, but nonetheless a solution or answer flashes before our eyes. In the movie *Hook*, the character named Smee, played by Bob Hoskins, says to Captain Hook rather abruptly, "I've just had an apostrophe."

Dustin Hoffman, as the captain, replies dryly, "I think you mean epiphany."

Smee nods without acknowledging his mistake and continues, "Lightning has just struck my brain."

Often the "ah-ha" moment hits us suddenly and without warning, like lightning flashing down from some mysterious place high above. We are suddenly aware of a truth that had previously never crossed our mind.

These two types of "ah-ha" moments—one sudden and bestowed on us by the fates, the other hard-earned—are distinct and different. But one unfortunate truth links them: People often fail to respond adequately to both of them. Once those flashes of insight have occurred, they are often left behind and too soon forgotten. To continue with our movie analogy, what if Eliza, having learned the tricks of disguising her accent, reverted back to her old ways the next morning? What if she failed to implement her new skills in her meetings with high-society people? Why do many people fail to respond properly to their "ah-ha!" moment? Why do these experiences often remain novel and isolated moments and not something that transforms our whole approach to life?

TRAPPING INSIGHT, UNDERSTANDING LEARNING

A popular exercise in many classrooms these days is to have students diagnose what types of learners they are. The following diagram* shows the various types of learning.

---

* PB Works website, http://introductiononlinepedagogy.pbworks.com/f/1242154 232/1242154232/01F1.1_R2D2%20components.jpg.

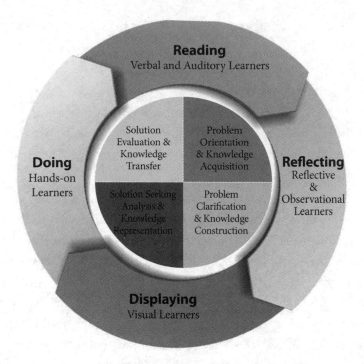

Students are encouraged to figure out what sort of learner they are so that they can approach their homework and individually differentiated assignments in the most productive way possible. Other scholars break the three types of learners into auditory, visual, and kinesthetic. In that framework, an auditory student can read something over and over again, but he won't actually *get* the concept until he hears it. Or, to be a bit more nuanced, he might *get* something that he *hears* much more quickly than he would when *reading* the same material. All of this may beg the question: Who cares? To some extent, reading is going to happen in school. What good do these diagnoses do? Well, with this information, students are also asked to be aware when something is a weakness. They can take steps to mitigate that weakness. But by knowing their weaknesses, they are better able to leverage their strengths. An auditory learner can ask a parent to read a poem to her at the dinner table or read it out loud herself. A kinesthetic learner can use Play-Doh® to learn visually and work through a tricky mathematical or scientific concept. Once you think about how you learn, you might be better prepared to more deeply understand and know your insight.

When we think of insight as a wake-up call, it is helpful to think of the way we learn. Learning and processing a certain new understanding of things isn't a singular process. It takes time and effort to refine that knowledge. We have to deepen it and figure out how it applies in various practical settings. Our character Eliza could do nothing better, if she wanted to maintain that fancy accent, than to practice it in real settings, to spend time with people who do that accent correctly. She needs to use her learning to keep it.

I hope I don't have to convince you that, at times, the most valuable insights are lost and remain unimplemented. Robert Sutton and Jeffrey Pfeffer wrote an excellent book, *The Knowing–Doing Gap*, about just this thing. They argue that traversing this gap is essential for business success, but that too often we substitute talk for action. These authors argue that "learning by doing" is almost always a more valuable and deep form of learning than "learning by listening" or "learning by reading."* If you haven't read that book, it is a good thing to consider when you are trying to leverage your wake-up call of insight. In the interim, consider the following obstacles that prevent you from taking your insight from knowing to doing.

My personal experience in working with leaders has convinced me that there are four trap doors that limit the potential of a moment of insight. We have to be prepared to respond to each of these potential

---

* Jeffrey Pfeffer and Robert I. Sutton, *The Knowing–Doing Gap: How Smart Companies Turn Knowledge into Action* (Boston: Harvard Business School Press, 2000).

pitfalls to maximize the insights for which we've worked and those insights that have just come to us mysteriously from above.

1. Procrastination

I heard some great news recently. Researchers at a major university have discovered the cure for procrastination…they will be revealing their findings at some undetermined date in the future. This is a funny little joke, but it holds some sad elements of truth. The problem of procrastination is so widespread that it is easy to imagine even those who research it falling prey as well. Nobody is a committed procrastinator, but many are faithful practitioners. All of us have elements of procrastination, for sure. Unfortunately, procrastination can be one of the primary enemies of insight.

The main reason for this destructive force is nothing more than the tyranny of our existing habits. It is not that we are habitual procrastinators; it is that our habits allow us to procrastinate. Perhaps we don't have enough spare time built into our days. Often we are too harried to act on our insights. Instructive here is the practice of John Wooden, perhaps the greatest college basketball coach in history. On the first day of practice, he'd take his highly regarded UCLA players—Lew Alcindor, Bill Walton, and Gail Goodrich— and teach them to tie their shoes.

There was a method to this madness. Wooden believed players had to start with good habits so that they were prepared to act in the game. Basketball is a great deal about improvisation and quick responses. Players must react to their opponents in real time and adjust their motions to play defense or attempt a play on offense. They must move to defend a pass and shift to help a teammate. And they have to do all those things very quickly. It is hard to do those things when your shoes are untied! We have to make sure we have structures in place so that we can respond quickly. We should not be caught tying our shoes when we should be looking to score.

Insight typically will come to us at a moment when we least expect it. We may be working on one project with a specific set of expectations, and an unanticipated breakthrough opens up possibilities in a different arena. We may be struggling to initiate a program when we suddenly have a great idea for a new one. The challenge we face is that our plans, agendas, and existing obligations prompt us to put this insight on a back burner until we have time to devote to this new idea. We must be careful about allowing our patterns to trump the power of insight. The tendency of the procrastinator in these situations would be to put these new ideas off for a while: "I'll get to it later," people too often say. Later is almost never the right time for capturing the benefits of a unique insight. Now is almost always better. The most innovative companies build insight and innovation into goal structures. General Electric set goals for its design teams: A certain percentage of revenues needed to come from new ideas and technologies. The old model was working when GE set those goals. But they knew that markets shifted. They knew they needed to put systems in place that demanded innovation rather than hoping for it. You have to build systems that allow for, and perhaps even demand, innovation and insight. Where would Apple be if the company had stopped at the iPod? Figure out a way to build time into your schedule for pursuing insights. Don't put ideas off. When the wake-up call of insight rings in your head, now is better than later to answer it.

2. Perfection

For this second common pitfall, I can turn to thinkers who are typically regarded as having a bit more gravitas than musicals and kids' movies about Peter Pan. Voltaire famously argued that the "perfect," or "best," is "the enemy of the good." Voltaire wasn't alone in this argument. Plato and Socrates, long before him, argued for something called the "golden mean." This concept was one of a desirable middle between extremes. The wake-up call rarely comes as a complete/perfect thought. Usually, there are problems with it. The best way to describe insights, in fact, is a *new, and probably incomplete, level of clarity*. These calls involve new understandings, a new vision, or a new route that was previously unclear or hidden.

Insight is usually an invitation to take further steps, to redirect time and attention. It is usually *not* a perfected product. I'll come back to Apple again and again in this book. Steve Jobs's insights were pretty broad; he believed that products should be simple and attractive. From these principles came his maniacal demand for innovation after innovation. From that notion came his focus on the touch screen that now comes standard on many of our devices. He didn't have one idea in his head; he had principles of insight that led to products.

Jobs is a uniquely positive example in this case. Most leaders with perfectionistic tendencies can dismiss the gift of insight as a distraction that is perhaps a bit too whimsical. How easy would it have been for the struggling computer engineer, as he demanded that his new computer be unique and easy to use, to give up and cede the tech world to IBM? Insight is an opportunity to perfect, not to reveal perfection.

When we fall through the trap of perfection, we may delay our claim on insights until it is too late. I have always been fascinated by the story that Alexander Graham Bell and Elisha Gray both developed the technology for "electrified communication" (more commonly known to today's world as the telephone) at relatively the same time and in the same exact city. But how many people have heard of Elisha Gray? How many phone companies are named after him? Bell's name is the one we know, largely because of the way he responded to his insight. His immediate reaction when he heard the sounds coming across the wire was to jump up and down in excitement. But Bell also had the mechanisms in place to get his patents *before* he was actually through with his inventions. He knew that getting to the starting line first was more important than getting there with a perfect product. Ten years later, Bell was an extremely rich man. Do you dwell on perfection or jump to act as soon as you should?

3. Protection and Fear

Another obstacle to capturing the value of insights is less about unintentional neglect—procrastination—and more about uncontrollable emotion—fear. On Friday nights, I watch the television show "Shark Tank" with my thirteen-year-old son. For those of you who are not familiar with the show, contestants come before a panel of investors ("sharks") and try to "sell" their ideas to possible funders or venture capitalists. Weird thing to watch with a thirteen-year-old, you say? I am planting the seeds of entrepreneurship early in his life! Anyway, in one episode, a particular inventor caught my attention. The entrepreneur was appealing for venture capital on a product that he steadfastly refused to get patented. This led to difficulties in his interview—difficulties that were caught on the screen.

The "sharks" were interested in investing, but were clear in their discussions to him that he would be fired immediately if they did take an ownership stake. The inventor argued that if he got the patent, he would be at more risk of his precious idea being stolen. He was probably right. When you have a great idea and share it with the world, people will inevitably borrow from it. But the investors knew what too many timid inventors fail to grasp: The idea is worthless until you take the risk. They were not going to invest in a company or idea whose originator was defensive and unwilling to try for the big thing. You've surely heard the expression, "You've got to spend money to make money." The essence of this concept, in this chapter, rings particularly true. Once you've had the "ah-ha!"

moment of insight, you'd best be brave enough to put it out into the world. "Protecting" your insight simply means that it benefits nobody. Ironically, by hunkering down in protective mode, you run the risk of metaphorical starvation.

There are other versions of this "protecting" problem. At times, individuals worry about the changes an insight will necessitate. Sometimes people are so comfortable in one particular role that they avoid rocking their proverbial boat with possible changes. They are paralyzed by fear and seek only to protect the status quo.

4. Personal Experiences

I think the primary problem in conceptions of insight is that they are "personal" experiences. This can mean different things. At times, insights feel like awakenings that are private or applicable only in one's own unique situation. A business leader might have some insight about streamlining production processes, but then dismiss it as a personal preference or idea that couldn't work for others. On a more humorous and practical level, sometimes insights just happen in private moments. I've heard countless people claim that they have the best ideas in the shower! Popular myth holds that Martin Luther had the idea for his "Ninety-Five Theses" while sitting on the porcelain throne!

What gets our attention is personal. Therefore, we can mistakenly treat our "ah-ha!" moment as a personal and private thing not worth mentioning to a broader network. To pull from one of the more famous moments in US history, a story goes that Martin Luther King, Jr., wasn't planning on going into his "I Have a Dream" bit in Washington during the civil-rights march. But gospel singer and civil-rights activist Mahalia Jackson, who sang during the event, whispered into his ear beforehand, "Tell them about the dream, Martin." He'd shared that verbiage in private conversations but was unprepared to say it on such a grand stage. I'd suspect and argue that the purpose and the power of these individual moments of insight—however personal and private they may feel—do not benefit you alone.

What to Do Now?

Those are the four main barriers (all of which conveniently start with "p"!) that keep us from adequately addressing our insights. At times, we put things off to deal with others. On other occasions, we spend too much time worrying about perfecting things and too little time capitalizing on them. In the worst of instances, we worry so much about the possible risks posed by an insight that we keep quiet. Last, we sometimes mistakenly believe that insights won't apply to others. In each of those instances, we fail to take advantage of "ah-ha!" moments.

I may have convinced you, in this chapter, that these four particular pitfalls limit us from benefiting from "ah-ha!" insights. I may even have made you want to go back and watch *My Fair Lady*. But I haven't done a whole lot yet to tell you how to *avoid* those pitfalls. Once we know where the trap doors are, how can we avoid them? The solutions are actually pretty simple. To help answer that question, allow me to borrow heavily from the world of fire safety. If you are caught on fire with the flames of insight, there are three simple actions you must immediately take: Stop, drop, and roll!

Stop

The blinding flash of the obvious should function like a lightning bolt striking along your path. Stop what you are doing and give it your full attention. Do not dismiss this wake-up call by attempting to integrate it into your existing routine. Wake-up calls by their very nature are designed to move you from one activity to another. As it relates to insight, stopping simply means, "Give it your full attention." I've often heard religious people describe one purpose of church as a practical point of interruption. The idea is that, by setting aside some required time on Sunday, you are forced to step outside of your weekly thoughts, to slow down and focus on something else for a while. Allow insights to disrupt your schedule, disturb your habits, and disconnect your existing obligations. Put off your "normal" obligations for the opportunity of the new.

Drop

Once you have given a wake-up call your full attention, you must find a way to capture it and preserve it for future use. Get out your iPad and take notes, use your iPhone to record a voice memo, or if necessary, find your child's Etch-a-Sketch® to illustrate the design! For some people, this is not the most efficient way of taking notes. My point is to use what you have. I once heard a poet say that his best ideas inevitably came to him while he was sitting in traffic. He'd take out a napkin, write down a phrase or two, and put that napkin in his shirt pocket or wallet. Then he had the phrasing, or the seeds of a bigger idea, to use later. Whatever you do, employ some medium to capture the insight immediately. At times, it will look like a flow chart, sometimes it will be a formula, and sometimes it may be a series of words. Just make sure you get it out of your head and into the world! Document your insight in any form that is immediately available.

Roll

The scariest part of answering a wake-up call, for many people, is when you "go public." Failure on a private scale is bad enough. The prospect of failing or having an idea dismissed by others is far worse. Those possible fears or hesitations acknowledged, I am convinced that at some point, the clarity of your idea will need to be processed with somebody. To use our fire terminology, you'll need to get down on the ground of reality and move! Your idea may need to be processed with an expert in the field who will state, "You are crazy." It may require you to talk it through with somebody from a completely different discipline. Whoever it is, people who use their insights well use them to create networks and to serve as a starting point for questions. The most prolific inventor in American history, Thomas Edison, employed a group of "muckers," or invention assistants. He did not invent in a vacuum. He leaned on young college graduates and professionals to help him perfect his ideas. In fact, some historians consider his "research and development lab" his greatest invention of all.

THE FOUR "P'S" OF NETWORKING

I gave you four p's that typically restrain insight. As an extension of this "stop, drop, and roll" notion, perhaps the best prescription is to give you four p's of productive networking that might help you leverage your insight effectively. Edison's "muckers" are a great example of using others to maximize smaller insights in unique ways. I'd encourage you—when you receive the wake-up call of insight—to be aggressive in seeking outside opinions. Follow the four p's of networking:

1. **People:** Think about how others can add to your idea. Invite them to contribute in their own unique ways. Building a circle of interested colleagues and partners is perhaps the most valuable thing you can do to bring your insights into the real world.

2. **Possibilities:** As those people contribute, guide their contributions by encouraging them to think of the various possibilities for, and benefits and use of, your insight.

3. Purpose: Ask those people to help you clarify what purpose might help you sustain the value of your insight.

4. Public: Think broadly. What will be the value of this idea to the myriad constituencies out there in the public sphere?

The diagram below illustrates the desire of "insight" to break through barriers and shows how the four p's restrain the insight. Opposing pressure comes from the four forces: people (other important pieces of information), possibilities, purpose, and the public (the marketplace).

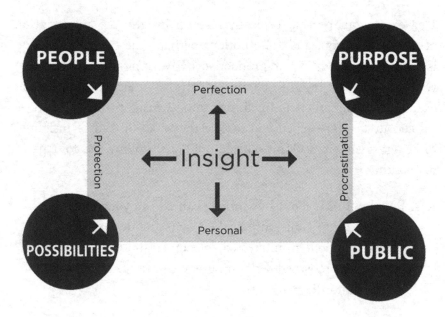

A REAL-WORLD EXAMPLE

I mentioned earlier one of my favorite clients, who was prone to exclaim that she'd had "a blinding flash of the obvious." What did her situation look like in reality? And how did she start to avoid the pitfalls of insight?

This client was an attorney in Boston. She'd worked for years for others but eventually started her firm from scratch in what Michael Gerber would call "an entrepreneurial seizure." She'd suddenly tired of all the problems she faced in her firm, all the inefficiencies and flawed policies. Like so many of us, she'd mused for years about how she *wished things were different.*

One day, out of the blue, she realized *she* could do things differently. But she'd need to start her own firm to do it. *I can start my own practice,* she thought, *and do this better.* For the next few months, she went about building a foundation for this idea. She followed the first principle—stop—and put some personal things on hold to pursue her dream. Next, when she was busy going about her day-to-day routine and had an idea about a business practice she hoped to implement, she followed the second principle—drop. She dropped what she was doing and jotted her idea down on a piece of paper. She sent herself e-mail reminders that pertained to her new venture to "Do X." Then she followed the third principle—roll. She rolled around in the real world. She didn't go it alone. She hired a coach (me) to help her improve her marketing and leadership skills, worked with consultants about her ideas, and opened up to feedback from her employees.

She then did a pretty "businessy" thing for a lawyer. She wrote a series of "nuts and bolts" guides for her target clients. She wanted to reach out to them and be prepared to answer their questions and apprehensions, to seize the initiative in that dynamic. She designed office systems to streamline delivery of services to clients. Her employees had checklists and protocols they were expected to follow, but she invited their feedback on methods to add efficiency. In general, she developed an "action orientation" that took the place of a "need to be perfect." She didn't have to do things perfectly. Her staff just needed to do things as well as they knew how. And they needed to do them often. They based their policies on the argument of *The Knowing–Doing Gap*, which argues for the power of "knowing by doing." And, in this particular instance, that form of "knowing" and "doing" turned out to be delightfully profitable.

CONCLUSION

In that scene I quoted earlier from *Hook*, after Smee exclaims to Captain Hook, "Lightning has just struck my brain!" Hook responds in deadpan, "That must hurt." It's a funny bit, but it's also true. Insights are rarely without their pains and difficulties. Avoiding the common pitfalls of insight are difficult. There is a reason that procrastination is the root of so many jokes. The search for perfection is a virtue that can quickly turn into a vice. Human beings are creatures who constantly seek to protect our own interests, and we can sometimes have a problem understanding how our own thoughts might apply to others. But if your insight will ever produce value in such a way that others benefit, it will require that you go public. There is a really popular TED Talk video called *When Ideas Have Sex*. The author argues that the single greatest advantage humanity has is our ability to specialize and to combine our specialization with that of others, the process of which raises everyone's living standards. The example he uses is that no one in the world can make a smartphone alone. The electrical engineer wouldn't be able to mine the materials or complete the design. The designer wouldn't be able to forge partnerships with phone companies and arrange for mass production in China. But combining specializations of all those people results in something remarkable.

When you share your insights with others, you make it more likely that you will enjoy the benefits of their insights as well. When we share our talents and skills, and when others join in this sharing, everyone's standard of living is raised. Trade, the speaker argues, "is ten times as old as farming." Human beings have been trading for a long time. Why not put your insights on the trading floor as well?

Be judicious about the first people you choose as a sounding board for your insight. Each time you share, you will enjoy increasing amounts of clarity. Along the way, others will add value to the initial flash of insight. Some will challenge your idea, and others will distract you from your initial purpose. No matter what, you must go public. So stop, drop, and roll. Then get up and get going! When you've experienced the wake-up call of insight, you have to answer it quickly and effectively.

CHAPTER 2

EUREKA!
THE WAKE-UP CALL
OF SUCCESS

"So be sure when you step, step with care and great tact. And remember that life's A Great Balancing Act. And will you succeed? Yes! You will, indeed! (98 and 3/4 percent guaranteed) Kid, you'll move mountains."
—DR. SEUSS, OH, THE PLACES YOU'LL GO!

WHEREAS THE LAST chapter described the kind of "wake-up" calls popularly depicted throughout culture, and that were probably quite easy to understand, this chapter is a bit different; it addresses "wake-up calls" that may feel counterintuitive. I will start with a couple examples. The first is from popular culture, and the second is from my own business experience. They share a common theme. Both are examples of wake up calls that went unheeded and led to disastrous results. But they are both events that, at first blush, were altogether positive. After discussing those examples, I'll move on to some of the dangers of success and will attempt to unpack the various ways in which your success should be treated appropriately. What is the right way to answer the wake-up call of success?

BIG-SCREEN DRAMA: HOLLYWOOD AS A DANGER ZONE

It's amazing what a difference a few years, and some bad personal decisions, can make in one's career arc. Just a few years ago, Lindsay Lohan was a star who could do no wrong. She was in successful remakes of *The Parent Trap* and *Freaky Friday*. She followed that up with *Herbie Fully Loaded* and *Mean Girls*. Perhaps most impressive to critics, she held her own on the screen next to Meryl Streep and Lily Tomlin in a movie version of *A Prairie Home Companion*. She was a Disney darling who had graced magazine covers. She had the life for which many young girls pine.

Today, her career has fallen into a tailspin. Movie stars never want to resort to cable TV, and she's had several cameos on shows of questionable quality. She has resorted to peddling cheap beauty products. This change in her job titles is largely the result of misbehaviors. Her mug shot has been plastered in more monthly magazines than anyone cares to count, she has let loose with outbursts in court, and she has undergone visits to rehab. One look at the list of child stars gone "bad" shows that Lohan is not alone. Lohan, Britney Spears, Michael Jackson, Danny Bonaduce, and the Olsen twins are just a few young stars who experienced great success and subsequently suffered terrible breakdowns. There are exceptions to this list, sure. But it certainly feels like there are more Lindsay Lohans than Ron Howards. Maybe the Lindsays just get more media coverage. Regardless, that sort of precipitous fall from grace is our first cautionary tale.

The next example comes from the experience of someone I met recently. Last summer, I had the good fortune to sit at a roundtable with a group of successful entrepreneurs. I listened to each of them as they shared their own secrets for success. I am always looking for common threads in those kinds of meetings. What sorts of things have these people done that might work for my clients? At that table, a woman who coached real estate agents in the Northeast told a story that captured my curiosity. She started to tell about some of her principles of investing. I listened politely, but was certainly not totally engaged. I was thinking of my work obligations coming up, or perhaps my dinner plans for the evening. Then, in an offhand and casual fashion, she happened to mention something highly unusual.

Five years earlier, this lady had won more than $50 million in the New York State Lottery. She didn't dwell much on the event, but that aside caught my ear. The meeting was soon over, and my interest was piqued. My curiosity prompted me to follow her out of the room and pelt her with dozens of questions. At first, she mentioned how lucky she'd felt to win such an amazing sum of money. But, as I asked a few more questions, she began to divulge just how the unplanned experience of coming into unusual monetary success had posed problems. It had almost destroyed her marriage, ruined her business, and killed her vision. She and her husband argued over finances as the pall of greed began to shade their interactions. She lost her capacity to exercise dutiful caution. She became an entirely different sort of—and much more reckless and ineffective—investor and manager of employees. Winning the lottery did not turn out to be a positive change in her life.

With these two examples in mind, I want to argue that success can be a profound "wake-up" call. This chapter lists some different types of success and the problems they have caused people. It addresses some of the science behind why success causes such issues. Then it gives recommendations for using success—not as a problematic destination, but as a promising beginning.

A SWORD CUTTING DAISIES

Tennessee Williams is one of the more famous playwrights the United States has ever produced. His plays—*Cat on a Hot Tin Roof, The Glass Menagerie, A Streetcar Named Desire*—are performed annually in local theaters and experience regular resurgences on Broadway. Williams's first big "hit" was *The Glass Menagerie*. With that success, he went from a small-town Mississippi boy to a nationally known figure. Then he wrote an essay that was published in *The New York Times* in 1947. In it, he lamented the "Catastrophe of Success" and argued that a person can be ruined by luxury and the vanities of wealth: "Once you know this is true, that the heart of man, his body, and his brain, are forged in a white-hot furnace for the purpose of conflict (the struggle of creation) and that with the conflict removed, the man is a sword cutting daisies, that not privation but luxury is the wolf at the door and that the fangs of this wolf are all the little vanities and conceits and laxities that Success is heir to—why, then with this knowledge you are at least in a position of knowing where danger lies."*

Williams is most certainly right. He worried about how much more deeply he felt the world when he was struggling, about how spoiled he'd get once he was highly regarded and appreciated. Examples of this are rampant and run through just about every artist and culture in human history. The two stories with which I started this chapter are, unfortunately, representative of all-too-common themes. Professional athletes almost always perform better in a "contract year," or a year in which they are playing and anticipating the next big contract negotiation. Great authors often produce their best works when they

---

* John (forum participant), "The Catastrophe of Success by Tennessee Williams," True. Good. Beautiful. website, last modified September 10, 2009, http://truegoodbeautiful.com/uncategorized/the-catastrophe-of-success-by-tennessee-williams/.

are young. Musicians almost always struggle with their "sophomore" album after enjoying immediate success with their debut album. Think of The Rolling Stones and Paul McCartney. They tour the country these days playing all their old hits. They rarely produce new ones.

SUCCESS EARNED, MOTIVATION CRUSHED

In each of the scenarios described above, people who had typically been lauded and praised fell prey to the danger Williams describes. Success and all its vanities ruined them. In the case of child actors, they spend their most formative years being protected and pampered. So they rarely learn how to do many of the practical things for themselves that almost all human beings know by the time they reach adulthood—things such as how to do the laundry, cook meals, schedule events, and pay bills. Worse, after standing in front of adoring fans so frequently, they lose the ability to socialize with peers who are equals. They are modern-day royalty, and royalty typically has problems associating with normal people. On the other side of the coin, those stars have been exposed to so many unique things that were probably beyond their maturity level. They were thrust into the fast-paced, high-intensity world of show business. How could they possibly be prepared for the tedium and monotony of a regular Monday without any high-energy activities on the agenda?

The real estate agent I mentioned in the beginning of this chapter offers another informative case. She was much better at her job when she had less room for error. Wealth has a way of leading to relaxed standards and expectations, as the stakes—whether something works or not—are so much lower. Who cares if a new business initiative works if you are going to have surf and turf and fine wine on the table the next night, regardless? This mindset leads to all sorts of problems in relationships with employees. If you can't understand or fully empathize with where people are coming from, you probably can't lead them well.

In their "contract years," athletes offer physical, but metaphorically apt, support for this theme. During those years, they typically come into training camp in better shape. They will play through nagging injuries that, if compensation isn't on the line, might have led them to sit out a game or two. They don't take plays off. In general, they give their best effort throughout the season. And then, once they get that multimillion-dollar contract, they hit the weights a bit less frequently. All of a sudden, they have that extra glass of wine at dinner the night before a game. Their ferocity suffers, and their performance follows suit.

I've read Daniel Pink's *Drive.* I know what neuroscience suggests about the importance of internal/intrinsic motivation. I believe that money often is not the best long-term motivational tool. But I also know that success can lead to some negative traits. What can we do to watch out for those traits and avoid them? Let's take one more detour before we address the answer to that question.

In August 1896, three men discovered gold in "them thar hills" on the banks of the Klondike River in Alaska. It is estimated that almost thirty thousand people took the treacherous journey through the passes of the Alaskan wilderness to strike their fortune and pan for gold. Jack London (one of the Klondike gold rushers) estimates that prospectors spent about $220 million in cumulative dollars to search for what turned out to be $22 million in gold.

Imagine today an untapped community receiving a $220 million infusion of capital and thirty thousand new residents requiring services. In the town of Dyea, Alaska, the population boom gave rise to 150 new businesses, including 48 hotels and 2 hospitals. Of course, only a few prospectors were wildly successful, but a multimillion-dollar industry was birthed, and entrepreneurship was on fire.

Certainly the effects of this kind of success would be a platform that future successes could be built on. Certainly towns such as Dyea, Alaska, are still thriving today, especially after the discovery of oil and timber would fuel the industrial revolution. Actually, by 1903, the population of this gold-rush town was a mere three people, and all businesses were closed.

Today, Skagway, Alaska, remains the only population center along the Klondike, and its primary industry is tourism from the cruise lines bringing passengers who are in the mood to buy jewelry. What happens that allows for "busts" to follow such "booms" in territories and individuals? What are the dynamics that limit sustainable performance in the aftermath of success? Once those child stars and athletes we discussed earlier experience initial success, once you've enjoyed your first major victories in the business world, how can you make sure that your "boom" leads to sustained growth rather than a "bust" of personal failure?

RELATIVE SUCCESS ISN'T THE ENDGAME

Like the ambitious prospectors who risked it all in an effort to pan for gold, those who aspire to leadership are willing to make sacrifices to achieve personal and organizational success. Often, they delay family obligations or personal goals to pursue professional growth. They will put in the long hours that success necessitates. I'm sure that Bill Gates had his share of all-night programming sessions, his share of twenty-hour days. Perhaps one of the riskiest moments in the journey is when a person achieves his first taste of what he would define as "success." It seems that first experience of success often sends the brain a message: "Relax, you made it!" The by-products of that advice are as follows: You can stop trying, stop growing, stop pursuing. It's a tempting proposition. *I've worked hard enough*, you say. *I've earned some time off*, you might think. If you stop long enough, maybe you can hear the faint sound of an alarm, letting you know it is time to wake up and keep pressing forward.

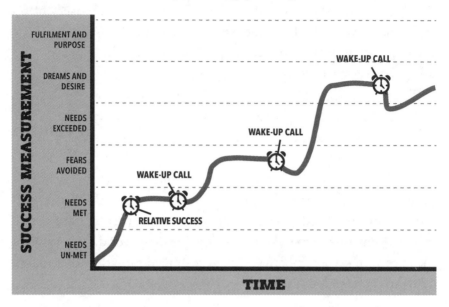

Take a look at the graphic above. It depicts the story of so many of our lives, the idea that we move gradually up the stages-of-success plateaus. First, we relish the pleasure of having met our needs. Our business may have succeeded to the point of paying the bills. We may have started to cash in, slowly but surely, and actually pay ourselves. This is the "Fears avoided, needs met" stage. When we reach this stage, we breathe a huge sigh of relief. No longer do we have to worry about which bill to pay this month. No longer do we have to explain to employees that, if they stick with us, rewards *eventually* will come.

The entrepreneur who reaches the next stage, "Needs exceeded," reaches another sort of plateau. She might start to buy stuff for her loved ones or splurge occasionally after years of bootstrapping it. This is the stage at which many of us go on trips or reward ourselves with a few fabulous meals or some time off. We need to ensure that this brief period of success doesn't become a plateau on which we grow too satisfied. Allow me to ask you a series of provocative questions:

- What was your first taste of professional success?
- How did you measure it?
- How did you respond to the experience?
- What happened next?

Do you think the answers to those questions would have been the same had you not been hungry for victory, thirsty for the feeling of triumph? Once you had the first taste, did you grow thirsty for more? The two most common by-products of success, I believe, are complacency and arrogance.

Complacency is well depicted in the graphic we just discussed. Once you've reached a certain level of success, it is tempting to call the view great and the journey over. It is harder, once you've reached a certain level, to want to keep climbing. After all, climbing is hard! But you have to figure out a way to remember that the view is always better from higher up. You have to understand that the view from that plateau might eventually grow old, but that if you lose momentum, it'll be harder to climb higher and higher later on.

Tragically, the overwhelming majority of people achieve a success plateau and stay there. Similar dynamics that affect the wake-up call of insight are influential in keeping people on a success plateau longer than necessary or healthy. Procrastination, perfection, protection, and personal experiences conspire to make our time on the success plateau seem natural, appropriate, and safe.

Success plateaus serve a purpose. They allow us to rest, recover, and reflect. Time on a success plateau allows us to interpret the events that have led to our success. While enjoying a plateau, we can lay the groundwork for further pursuits.

To get off of the various stages of the success plateau, there are certain events, or "wake-up calls," that should serve you. Certainly, you should enjoy your victories when they come. We need to hear the phone ring when specific events occur that are designed for us to move further up the success ladder. Often these "wake-up calls" are interpreted as threats, but they are intended for us to move on to greater motivators.

To get "unstuck" from the plateau requires that you tap into more powerful motivators. These motivators must replace the basic desires of simply having our needs met, avoiding the things we fear, and possibly having our needs exceeded. The wake-up calls encountered while resting on a success plateau invite us to explore our deepest dreams and clarify our greater purpose.

The alternative graphic below illustrates how getting "unstuck" will require a risky step down from the plateau before we can progress up to a level of greater success. Ironically, greater success often does not involve money and things. We must begin to recognize that greater success involves meaning and purpose.

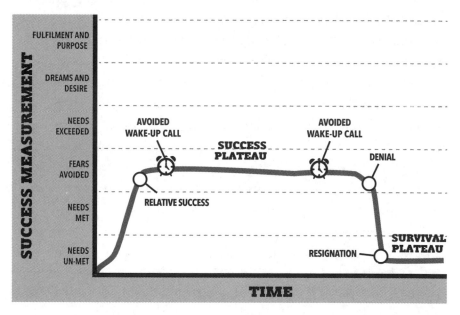

I'd argue that there are four "wake-up calls" that can happen while we are languishing or relaxing on that "success plateau":

1. **A competitor surpasses your performance**—Ask Ford and GM right now if their old plateau—control of the American car market—was as safe and secure as they thought. While they dwelled on their old model, comfortable in their success, Toyota and Nissan gained ground year after year. Just a few years ago, that plateau was pretty close to a grave. Now, the American car manufacturers are once again struggling to reach even the most cursory levels of success—namely, regular profitability.

2. **You lose the enjoyment of leadership**—When leaders stop caring about going to work, stop waking up energized, there is no way they can be as effective as they were before. I always encourage leaders who have lost the thrill of the job to take some time away, to reflect, to find their passion again. That plateau of success can't sustain you when you aren't looking to climb farther.

3. **You become bored**—Getting an enterprise off the ground can be an adrenaline-filled adventure. The success plateau can serve the purpose of helping the body and mind recover from hormones pulsating through the entrepreneur's veins. If the recovery lingers for too long, the disease of boredom could kick in, and the entrepreneurial leader might go shopping for distractions to replace the rush. Famously, Lee Iacocca, who started out so successfully at Chrysler, got involved in all sorts of distracting endeavors that later limited

his efficacy and adversely impacted his objectivity. As he got involved in politics and bought Italian villas, his leadership at Chrysler suffered terribly.

4. **You become susceptible to irrelevant distractions**—If you've ever watched a child who has just learned to walk, it is amazing how quickly she moves from one distraction to the next. "This ball is interesting...but not as interesting as that book.... Wow, that box of blocks looks great!" There are lots of reasons that children would make bad employees, but this lack of ability to focus on what matters has to be one of the most important. Good leaders who are capable of taking their organizations to the next stage of success are able to "filter out all the noise," to use famous statistician Nate Silver's phrase, and to search only for the right signal!

The second main problem that can lead to "relative" success is the tendency and temptation toward arrogance. Arrogance will establish a limited effectiveness in leadership. In my first book, *Wide-Awake Leadership*, we dedicated an entire chapter to the risks associated with the arrogance that success can produce. The essence of that argument, made here, is about the absolute need for humility. I've often been fascinated with sports teams that enjoy great success, but struggle the next year to replicate it, even with the same staff. Reports come out during the preseason about particular players who came into training camp a bit heavier than the previous season. They might have enjoyed too much wine and relaxation in celebration! Moving to the next level of success means knowing when to relish victories and when to put those victories in the rear-view mirror and to set newer, better goals.

The Process Is More Important than the Result!

When I was a young father, I would swing my young daughter by her arms. She would giggle and say the words every father loves to hear: "Do it again, Daddy!" Imagine if my response had been, "You have already laughed and had your fun. I have no idea how to do it again." One of the most important gifts in life is figuring out how to repeat doing something that you have discovered works. In this setting, we want to figure out how—once we've experienced personal and professional successes—to replicate those successes. At the same time, as our focus on the "success plateau" above emphasizes, you have to balance the capacity to replicate results with a thirst for, and acceptance of, new ideas and opportunities.

There is no arguing that results do matter, but when you focus on the process, you establish a pattern for sustainable success. You hear this all the time from coaches of successful college football teams. Before a big rivalry, when interviewed about the emotional day, the coach will say, "We just want everyone to focus on doing his particular job." That coach might also try to temper the focus on how "important" the game actually is by claiming, "This is a game, like any game. It counts the same on our record as last week's game against Po-Dunk State. We are going to take it one play at a time."

People can roll their eyes at this "coach speak," but it points to an important truth. You have to focus on the minute levels of process to get meta-results. An exaggerated emphasis on results might promote shortcuts, unethical behavior, and possibly bad habits. The most important aspect of sustaining success is repeating the processes that initially yielded positives in the first place. What were the steps you took? How did you prepare for the big meeting? What did you do the night before a major rollout? Why were you successful? Can you repeat that formula?

REMEMBER, THE RIGOR IS MORE IMPORTANT THAN THE FORMULA!

Often, I think of a story a friend told me about his church. The recruiting committee at his church had concerns about the lack of young people attending the Sunday services. So they got together a group of their younger members and asked them a question: "What kind of church would people who have never been to church attend?" Because the young members were *not* those kind of people, they felt ill-equipped to answer the question. So they did something smart.

To discover the answer to this question, they went door-to-door asking people if they went to church. If the answer was "yes," they thanked the person at the door and moved on. When they came upon somebody who didn't attend, they respectfully asked what sort of things would get this respondent to attend. They recorded all of the responses, grouped them thematically, and designed a church accordingly. The results of their efforts birthed one of the largest churches in North America, with weekend attendance exceeding 20,000, and started a modern-day reformation.

The formula their research yielded influenced armies of churches across America. Some of these churches were moderately effective. But most churches floundered in their desire to be relevant to people with no church background. In attempting to use the initial discoveries and replicate the model, those struggling churches failed to understand that sometimes the results are more a reflection of the investment of energy than the simple data that are gleaned. *Sustainable success is often about the rigor we employ in the pursuit of our success formula.*

STAY HUNGRY, RESIST SATISFACTION!

Attorney John Morgan recently released a book outlining his reflections on his success and the future of the practice of law. The title of his book—*You Can't Teach Hungry!*—is good food for thought for this chapter. Among the first attorneys in the country to advertise his expertise to victims of automobile accidents, Morgan was dismissed by his fellow lawyers as an "ambulance chaser." Those old-school lawyers stayed rooted in their old model. They believed clients would come knocking when they needed something. They failed to reach out proactively to recruit new clients, to forge new markets for themselves. Now those same attorneys turn to Morgan for guidance and strategies. John discusses in his book the impact that "hunger" had on him as a young lawyer. It drove him toward innovative tactics and motivated him to work harder than the next guy. Hunger was a big part of his success.

I want to argue in this book, without disagreeing with my friend John, about the importance of staying hungry. You might not be able to teach hunger. But, for many people, hunger is all too easily satisfied. Too many people settle for the mediocrity of short-term success. They are more enamored with fixing their hunger than seeking greater success and fulfillment. Hunger does not need to be taught and perhaps can't be. What does need to be taught is that success is almost always rooted in passion. And somehow, people have to summon up a capacity to maintain dimensions of their hunger for future projects.

I heard a really strange interview with Kanye West the other day. For those of you who don't know, West is a sometimes-unsavory music producer and performer. In using him as a reference, I am in no way endorsing his behaviors or art. But he did some things that struck me as interesting.

In this interview, West was talking about his aspirations to enter the world of fashion. He talked a bit about his ideas for new trends and clothing lines. One of them was leather sweatpants. I don't even understand how that could be a marketable idea. But, as West talked, he soon became more and more furious that the world wasn't respectful of this great idea he had. This man has reached levels of success that most of us will never know. He has plenty of money to retire. But there he was, furious at some perceived slight about an altogether strange idea.

So many great teams and successful individuals find a way to stay motivated. Often, they do this by convincing themselves that "no one believes in me," or "people don't respect me enough." How can you spark your own hunger for more? How can you motivate yourself even in the face of success?

STAY HUMBLE

Kanye West and John Morgan found ways to stay motivated and hungry. Later, I will address the example of Michael Jordan, who did much the same thing. These entrepreneurs found ways to convince themselves that others still didn't believe in them. This is one dimension of a broader approach to maintaining success. Often, individuals can't stay humble. They greet power and success, eventually, as if they really and truly deserved it. If you experience enough success, soon enough you talk yourself into the idea that you deserve that success more than other people. Percy Shelley's great sonnet *Ozymandias* addresses this topic:

> And on the pedestal these words appear:
> 'My name is Ozymandias, king of kings:
> Look on my works, ye Mighty, and despair!'

Nothing beside remains.
Round the decay
Of that colossal wreck, boundless and bare
The lone and level sands stretch far away.

Shelley is mocking the pride and hubris of this great king. The king thought he could defeat death and maintain his glory throughout eternity. But all signs of his "might" were defeated by the sands of time. It is a terrible thing to overestimate your own victories. In the process, you can forget about all of the things—outside of your own control—that contributed to them. Did your parents send you to great schools, thus ensuring that you were better positioned for a good first job? Did they teach you to value education or drive you to the extra practice, even when they were tired? Were you born with a special gift that perhaps others don't have? Did you have a unique teacher who got you started down a particularly fruitful path? By remembering these types of advantages, you can better remember just how much of your success was outside of your control. You can make choices about what sort of monuments might last longest. Stay humble! It'll better prepare you to help others, and it will keep you moving forward.

We've discussed some actors who struggled with success. Maybe it's time to mention an actor who has dealt with the pitfalls of success pretty well. Jon Hamm—better known as Don Draper of "Mad Men" fame—often mentions in interviews the years he struggled to get a foot in the door of show business. He lived in LA for years, worked as a waiter, and took really unglamorous roles just to pay the bills. He developed the kinds of friendships during those years that were based on real connections and a common bond forged in the fires of struggle.

Finally, when Hamm was cast in the show "Mad Men" for an upstart channel called AMC, he got his break. Within the span of a couple of short years, he went from being a waiter in a dive diner to being a Golden Globe winner, an Emmy nominee, and according to some glossy magazines, the "world's sexiest man." What has Hamm done with his success? He's maintained his relationships. His friends are the kind who will still rib him about his idiosyncrasies. They'll keep him rooted. They won't "yes" him into mistakes. When he's doing something that merits criticism, they'll criticize him and help him avoid hubris. Hamm has made a big deal about maintaining those relationships, about proactively preserving friendships with people who cared about him before he was a big thing. Will he experience moments of frustration with those friends, nights when he wishes they'd just go along with his argument? Sure. But real friendships are full of pushing and pulling; they are all bound together with frustrations and petty disagreements. By choosing to endure those dimensions of real relationships rather than simply search out a posse of "yes men," Hamm is situating himself for long-term sanity and success.

What will keep you rooted but hungry at the same time?

Example from the Field

My experiences with clients struggling to adjust to success are perhaps more rare than other types of interactions. But I've had some real-world experience with people who have failed to adjust properly to new opportunities, who have failed to answer the wake-up call of their own success. One particular client merits discussion here. Let's call him Joe.

Joe had checked all the boxes necessary for success. He'd done well in college. He'd gone straight on to pursue his graduate degree. Those diplomas in hand, Joe immediately landed an excellent job at a utilities company. Because of his education and training, Joe advanced quickly in that company. He worked extremely hard, demanded that things be done correctly on his watch, did his tasks on time, and was generally a model employee. Soon enough, he moved up a level to middle management. This transition was troubled from the start. As soon as he started managing others, Joe came to a terrible realization: Not everyone in the company was as effective and responsible as he was.

Joe responded to this realization in typical ways that are particularly problematic. He began to circle around to watch over people's shoulders, ensuring that they did everything the right way. Eventually, he began to do their jobs for them. When they realized what was happening, some were happy enough to cede responsibility. This made more work for Joe. He grew busier and less effective at everything he did. He grew obsessive and less diplomatic. Soon enough, Joe grew angrier.

If you're reading this business book, you're probably familiar with the "Peter Principle." In case you've forgotten, this principle states that members of an organization where promotion is based on achievement, success, and merit eventually will be promoted beyond their level of ability. They'll be promoted to the level at which they reach "incompetence." Was this an example of the Peter Principle in action? Did Joe's company incorrectly assume he'd be management material simply because he was a good employee in a lower position?

My discussions with people at Joe's company about this problem revealed that they didn't think so. They believed he was capable of doing really great things and were not ready to give up on him. They wanted to invest in his talent. So they called me. As I talked with Joe, I started to notice an overarching problem: He believed that his job was to "get the job done right." What he didn't understand, yet, was that management's role isn't just to ensure that things get done correctly. Does quality matter? Absolutely. But management's role is also ensuring that *things get done correctly by other employees.*

By going behind people and doing their jobs for them, Joe was doing *precisely* the wrong thing. I urged him to let go, just a bit, of his obsession with "quality." For a while, he needed to focus on empowering other people to fulfill their roles, even if the products produced weren't absolutely perfect. Once you've established relationships with your employees, once you've worked with them toward a mutual expectation of quality, then you can start to raise the bar of expectations. If you do that too abruptly, though, all you are going to get is a bunch of turnover and lack of quality.

Joe is a cautionary tale for another danger of success. Sometimes the formula for success at one level can be the recipe for destruction at another. Obsession with details at one level can be productive. But it can be problematic when your primary obligation is working well with people.

Conclusion

If you've achieved a level of success in your business and professional life, congratulations! Success is fun, and it serves as an indication that you're on a good path. In the midst of appreciating your initial accomplishment, let it also serve as a wake-up call. Tennessee Williams ends his essay with the argument, "The only somebody worth being is the solitary and unseen you that existed from your first breath and which is the sum of your actions."

What got you to that first taste of success? That formula is certainly worth considering. But, as Joe's story reminds us, sometimes you'll need to make changes in your approach to suit new settings and scenarios. In general, don't get too comfortable. Sustain the rigor you had before. Only that will yield continuous and sustainable growth.

This chapter leads nicely into the next, which is a variation on a similar theme. Difficulties managing the wake-up call of success bear plenty of resemblance to difficulties managing that most common metric of success: money and all the trappings that can come with it.

∽ CHAPTER 3 ∾

CHA-CHING!
THE WAKE-UP CALL
OF MONEY

Wealth without work
Pleasure without conscience
Science without humanity
Knowledge without character
Politics without principle
Commerce without morality
Worship without sacrifice
—Mahatma Gandhi's "Seven Deadly Sins"

Three researchers specializing in psychology and marketing collaborated in 2009 to publish an interesting set of findings in the *Journal for Psychological Science* titled "The Symbolic Power of Money: Reminders of Money Alter Social Distress and Physical Pain." The subtitle of the article clearly alludes to the argument that the mere idea of money can make people feel better socially and physically. With that basic fact in mind, you might anticipate that I'm going to make a positive argument about the impact that money can have when you're feeling defeated. The truth is a bit more complicated.

Zhou, Vohs, and Baumeister* employed a series of experiments to test the relationship between "money and interpersonal rejection." In other words, how might money mitigate the feeling of being isolated? The authors did some neat experiments. In one, they gathered some undergraduates and split them into same-sex groups of four. They offered those individuals a sum of money for participating. They had each group "get acquainted" for five minutes, after which they led them to separate rooms. The researchers described how the process worked as follows: "Each person indicated which group member he or she would like to work with on an upcoming dyad task. Then the experimenter returned to each participant and, by random assignment, said that either everyone (acceptance condition) or no one (rejection condition) had selected the participant and that this ostensible problem would preclude that participant from engaging in the dyad task."

The methods are a bit precise and lengthy to describe, but the essential element is this: Some people thought they'd been rejected, and some were led to believe that they were popular. The researchers then asked a series of questions that tested each participant's generosity. In short, participants grew greedier and less willing to donate money to charity when they were rejected. They tested worse on all three tests that measured their generosity. In another experiment, researchers found that thoughts of physical pain increased a desire for money. In still another, just thinking about money helped overcome distress and feelings of social isolation.

---

* Xinyue Zhou, Kathleen D. Vohs, and Roy F. Baumeister, "The Symbolic Power of Money: Reminders of Money Alter Social Distress and Physical Pain," *Psychological Science*, Association for Psychological Science, 2009, p. 700, posted on Carlson School of Management, University of Minnesota's website, http://www.carlsonschool.umn.edu/assets/127771.pdf.

Zhou, Vohs, and Baumeister conclude in their summary, "Money operates as a social resource that confers a broad, strong feeling of being able to cope with problems and satisfy one's needs. Resources are valued more in times of threat and adversity than at other times. Getting or having resources reduces pain and suffering; conversely, losing resources makes one more vulnerable, which intensifies suffering."

Why is this discussion of the psychological effects of money included in a book about wake-up calls? I probably could have just mentioned casually that money has powerful effects on people, and you would've nodded your head like a knowing reader, thinking back to all the times you'd been tempted to do something for money you otherwise wouldn't do. Alternatively, you could've remembered one of the many scandals you've heard about in the news that were motivated by greed for the all-powerful and all-precious green. You would've had plenty of anecdotal experience with the power that money, or the lack of it, can have on people. The scientific proof from the study above shows just how universal the drive for cash is, just how pervasive its influence can be on our minds and bodies. We all want it. It impacts our capacity for rational and clear thought about others. We all feel better when we have it. But what happens once we've gotten our hands on a significant amount?

Who better to tell us the answer to that question than 1980s pop icon Cyndi Lauper? The lyrics below are from her song, "Money Changes Everything":

> She said sorry baby I'm leaving you tonight
> I found someone new he's waitin' in the car outside
> [*To which a male answers*]
> Ah, honey how could you do it
> We swore each other everlasting love
> She said well yeah I know but when we did
> There is one thing we weren't thinking of and that's...."
> Money, money changes everything
> We think we know what we're doin'
> That don't mean a thing
> It's all in the past now
> Money changes everything

Lauper might have been guilty of some pretty aggressive 1980s fashion statements. Her hair color knew no bounds. Her clothing was an opus of neon and spandex clichés. But in these lyrics, she is spot on. Money has a way of changing everything. The research I started this chapter with points to a simple truth: Money messes with our minds. I might pose a controversial question here: Is money even a good thing?

Relax! This is a book for business leaders. It would be a pretty weird book indeed if I advocated for abandoning the monetary system as we know it. But the research on this question—Is money positive?—is fascinating. And the answer is...yes and no.

On the broadest possible level, you have to ask yourself about the effect that money has on performance. Steven Pink, in his work *Drive*, cites study after study proving that the promise of money as incentive can actually be detrimental to performance. In work that requires little ingenuity and creativity—such as on an assembly line, for instance—promises of better compensation can have a small impact on improved performance. But when tasks are complicated—like so many of yours are—the promise of additional compensation actually makes people perform *worse*. The explanations for this dip aren't entirely clear, but the results are. Suffice it to say, the promise of money is not going to make you any better at your job.

There are additional problems with money as well. One of those three researchers I cited earlier in this chapter, Kathleen Vohs, concluded in a 2006 study that money is bad for the interpersonal self.* In other words, wanting money has a counterproductive impact on relationships. It can tarnish friendships, cause tension in marriages, and break up families. Disputes can break out among spouses about what will be spent where. Character traits and values are tested. In short, money can cause significant damage to your relationships with others.

That same study, though, proves that money can be really positive for the personal self. Having money can make the difficulties of life much more manageable for individuals. In a world full of difficulty and sorrow, the individual needs all the help he or she can get! When you aren't worried about the daily bills, you can see the world's goodness much more clearly. To complicate things just a bit more, a more confident individual generally is going to be better at relationships. So let me make a suggestion that might help us approach money just a bit differently. I want to suggest that money— the presence or absence of it—is nothing more than a wake-up call. Let's look at some responses to money to gain clarity about the best way to answer the call when success comes calling.

LOTTERY WINNERS

I mentioned a woman in Chapter 2 who had been so lucky as to win the lottery. Her tale of those winnings almost destroying her interpersonal life was one I'd read about in the news. I wanted to do some digging to find out just how representative her story was. How

---

* "Kathleen Vohs," Social Psychology Network website, http://vohs.socialpsychology.org/.

many lottery winners actually *benefit* over the long term from their winnings? The National Endowment for Financial Education cites research estimating that 70 percent of people who suddenly receive a large sum of money will lose it within a few years.*

William "Bud" Post is a name that pops up as a cautionary tale for lottery winners. Mr. Post won $16.2 million in the Pennsylvania lottery in 1988. Today, he subsists on his Social Security checks of $450 a month. As he lost that fortune, ex-girlfriends sued him over a share of his winnings. His brother hired a hit man to kill him with the hopes of inheriting the winnings. At the bequest of those siblings who did not try to kill him, he made bad investments.

Although murder for hire is not typical, many elements of Bud Post's story are more common than you might think. When you look deeply into the majority of lottery winners, the results are dark. "Loan" requests from family and friends are almost universal, marital discord is common, and in a couple of stories, violence and drug problems led to a level of ruin that overshadows any possible benefits.**

ATHLETES

A particularly common form of lottery winner, albeit a form that is linked to skill and hard work, is the case of the modern-day professional athlete. Athletes frequently come from less-comfortable financial circumstances, and many are unprepared for the huge windfall that their talents and hard work earn them at a young age. They don't have the experience necessary to navigate great wealth. How

---

* "About 70 percent of Lottery Winners Go Broke," Neowin website, last modified February 24, 2013, http://www.neowin.net/forum/topic/1138272-about-70-percent-of-lottery-winners-go-broke/.
** Patricia Sullivan, "William 'Bud' Post III: Unhappy Lottery Winner," *The Washington Post* website, last modified January 20, 2006, http://www.washingtonpost.com/wp-dyn/content/article/2006/01/19/AR2006011903124.html.

many nineteen-year-olds, or twenty-four-year-olds for that matter, do you know who would cope well with millions? A 2012 ESPN documentary titled *Broke* profiled athletes who lost money to huge mansions, car collections, poor investment advice, and purchases as odd and exotic as pet tigers. A *Sports Illustrated* survey found that "78 percent of NFL players face bankruptcy or serious financial stress within just two years of leaving the game, and 60 percent of NBA players face the same dire results in five years." These are people who received multimillion-dollar bonuses, massive salaries, and additional sums of money from endorsements. These are people, in short, who make more money in a few short years than many people will make in their entire lives. But it is gone just as quickly as it comes in.

Antoine Walker, an NBA star who is somewhat criticized, played in the NBA for fifteen years and earned almost $110 million. Let me say that again—$110 million! In May 2010, Walker filed for bankruptcy. He blamed bad investments, but also had some problems gambling. In 2009, he was arrested and charged with writing $800,000 worth of bad checks to three Las Vegas casinos. He made terrible choices in real-estate investing. And Walker's isn't even the most egregious case. Former heavyweight boxing champion Mike Tyson is rumored to have squandered somewhere close to $400 million in less than twenty years. If you are wondering, he was also the one who purchased a tiger!

There are lots of reasons for these tragic numbers, and they go beyond ignorance and inexperience. Often, pro athletes do not seek professional financial and tax advice, often because they are concerned that some "professionals" may be in line for a handout as well. Others suffer from "ego bleed." Winners on the court or field can't fathom losing at anything. Some studies have shown, too, that athletes are just "wired differently.... Research found significant differences between athletes and nonathletes across personality characteristics such as inhibition, emotionality, and aggressiveness. Good characteristics on the field, but not necessarily optimum for making financial decisions."* Having spent their lives succeeding, when they are forced to enter a new world with financial stakes and tax implications they don't fully understand, athletes often find their lifetime fortunes squandered in a few short years.

So athletes and lottery winners are our bad examples. Many times, these groups of people come into massive amounts of money and find, upon retirement, that all of those earnings all too suddenly disappeared. Why does this happen for so many different types of people? Let's visit one of television's favorite families for some answers.

"THE BEVERLY HILLBILLIES"—NEW SCENE, OLD HABIT

From 1962 to 1971, television audiences were captivated by the story of a man named Jed Clampett. He struck oil on his property and went from not being able to keep his family fed to living in a Beverly Hills mansion. For nine seasons, the writers were able to explore, comically, the idea of coming into money without being fundamentally changed. This family moves to one of the most ostentatious places on earth. Beverly Hills has all the connotations of lavish wealth and glamour. And, when these mountain folks enter that universe, humorous conflict lurks around every interaction. The character known as Granny spends much of the series angry with some perceived slight by snobby city folk.

"The Beverly Hillbillies" represent, in broad strokes, many of the

---

* Robert Pagliarini, "Why Athletes Go Broke: The Myth of the Dumb Jock," CBS Money Watch website, last modified July 1, 2013, http://www.cbsnews.com/8301-505125_162-57591259/ why-athletes-go-broke-the-myth-of-the-dumb-jock/.

temptations newly rich people feel. They think they ought to live in the finest neighborhoods, eat at the best restaurants, and buy more expensive cars. People who've never had an interest in wine suddenly need wine cellars. People who drive ten miles to work on a highway suddenly need the same automobile used by the US military, Humvees, to make their commute. People who don't enjoy swimming pools all of a sudden *must have one*, replete with waterfalls. This pressure is largely self-inflicted and based on the competitive tendency in each of us.

We all want to "keep up with the Joneses" if we are remotely able. The "Hillbillies" are so fun to watch because they so regularly refuse to play the game. Sure, they've made the initial move, but they're still wearing overalls. They still speak with thick accents. They still suck on pieces of grass like your average country farmer. They continue to drive in the dilapidated old farm truck. The conflicts that arise in each episode are about class. Will the Hillbillies finally conform? Or will they maintain the values they had back before they struck oil?

All of us would like to believe that we know who we are. We all hope that we would not change if we had more money or less money. But rarely does that prove to be the case. The presence or absence of money often impacts with whom we talk and how we talk to them. Money shapes what we are able to do or not do with our spare time. Money shapes how we view others, reality, and ourselves. In short, the Hillbillies are all too rare. So each time you open your wallet or view your bank balance, if you listen, you might be able to hear your wake-up call. How should you respond to the changes of newfound monetary success?

To the World of Business

It's possible that you have enjoyed financial rewards after successfully navigating your particular business. There's no escaping the scorekeeping aspects of money in the life of entrepreneurs and executives. We're competitive people. It is what makes us get up so early in the morning and stay in the office so late. When we go to conventions, workshops, or other events with people in our industry, we compare notes on best practices. But we take those notes for more than our own edification. We want to learn more than how to do things differently. We also want to gauge where we stand compared to others who are respected. Such internal groups create a sort of greedy pecking order that leaves entrepreneurs and executives feeling better or worse than their peers. Often, I have clients who are perfectly comfortable with their status and business until they come back from one of these gatherings. All of a sudden, they fall prey to the tyranny of *more*.

During the past decade, I've coached hundreds of leaders. I've seen this trend play out countless times. The way leaders function is altered by financial rewards and incentives. Think of all the incentives that were in place for bankers before the financial crisis. In the mortgage industry, bankers started to package more and more "risky" assets in "safe" packages of subprime mortgages. These businesspeople were much less scared by the long-term implications than the short-term rewards. Eventually, the market drove a broader trend of lowered lending standards and higher-risk mortgage products. We all know what happened when that bubble burst. Many "successful" people hit rock bottom, and they unfortunately took others with them. You're not immune from that level of hubris and the problems that accompany it.

Ask yourself some questions:

- How have the financial rewards of my effective leadership impacted me?

- What were the behaviors, attitudes, practices, and beliefs that shaped my leadership trajectory early in my career?
- How have those changed over time?
- Has money altered them?

You might conclude that you have preserved the core of what got you where you are. In some ways, you might notice shifts that are for the better. You might be more cautious and frugal in your success, a positive thing. However, I'm willing to bet that there are some situations in which money has brought out attitudes, beliefs, behaviors, and practices that are incongruent with the core of who you are and who you want to be as a leader. They are probably subtle. An unnecessary expense here. A lavish choice there. I once talked to an executive who had chastised an assistant for buying him one of those new coffeemakers that makes individual cups. He didn't want to have *anything* at his disposal that the other employees didn't. He'd keep using the community coffee pot, thank you very much! No matter how big or small those changes might be, this is your wake-up call. Here are a couple of things to keep in mind as you try to build a foundation of sustainable practice in response to monetary success.

What to Do?

Many articles about what people who win the lottery should do are generic but helpful. They encourage lottery winners to "do nothing for a while," to take a breath and not make hasty decisions or investments. Alternatively, they suggest that winners spend some money wildly, but that they limit that reckless behavior to a small fraction of the total. They encourage winners to put their windfall in perspective: How many years of comfortable living could it fund at current expenses? How much can you leave your loved ones? Every lottery winner is encouraged to get professional advice, particularly when it comes to taxes. I'd second all of those recommendations for you in your professional life. But I also have a particular framework I'd like you to consider.

John Wesley served as a religious leader and cultural reformer during the mid-1700s. He spent much of his life wandering the new frontiers of America with his brother, Charles, spreading Christianity. The two are now considered the founders of Methodism. John Wesley offered this simple advice to the members of the movement he shaped: "Make all the money you can, save all the money you can, and give all the money you can." The Calvinists, who started this country, were passionate capitalists. But they also believed very specifically that material wealth and greed could drive you straight to the pits of hell. They are in many ways responsible for the charitable ethos of this country. With Wesley's advice in mind, and the example of those Calvinists, I suggest two responses to your wake-up call.

Make Your World Smaller

Leadership is a stressful endeavor. The challenges of allocating resources, clarifying your vision, and making tough decisions are unavoidably difficult. As a leader, it's imperative that you do not introduce unnecessary stress into your life by allowing money to control you. I've argued above that the presence or absence of money can be both positive and negative. We've seen some examples of people who've lost control of their egos and decision-making capacities in the face of money. And Jed Clampett has shown us, albeit fictionally, what it might look like to maintain your own character and qualities while also enjoying great wealth. This struggle with money is one that you must win if you are to keep stress in its proper perspective and to remain the kind of leader you want to be. How can you maintain that focus on what matters?

Practically speaking, what can a leader do to win that battle? There are timeless practices that promote our strength over the power that money can exert in our lives. You can make your world a lot less stressful by making your world a little smaller using the following disciplines:

1. **The practice of simplicity**—The most well-known example of this practice is found in the monk who takes a vow of poverty, who shuns material wealth for spiritual purity. But the practice of simplicity is not limited to monks who choose an obviously ascetic life. The practice of simplicity is not complex. Simply stated, it means to live within your means. And it means thinking critically about how lavish your means should be in the first place.

2. **The practice of saving**—This discipline can be destructive among those who get obsessive about hoarding. Even the king of savings, Dave Ramsey, encourages his listeners to spend on occasion, to maintain perspective when it comes to savings. With that disclaimer fully stated, it's important that one of your first actions with regard to wealth is to avoid spending before you allocate an appropriate percentage for savings.

3. **The practice of giving**—This discipline protects us from allowing money to control us and from living in the fear that we need to hoard. Before you keep and before you spend, find an avenue that is consistent with your core values. Choose to give to something bigger than yourself.

To take our discussion back to our example of athletes, think about how much better off those NBA players would be if they'd devoted money from their massive signing bonuses to savings. How much better off would they be if they'd chosen to buy a home in a moderate neighborhood rather than the ritziest one right on the ocean? How much more spiritually satisfied would they be if they'd given some of their windfall to causes that need financial help rather than to import-car dealerships? Is living like a rock star for a few years really worth decades of financial worry? By just using these three principles, I'd bet that fewer than 70 percent of those lottery winners would've squandered their winnings. And I think it makes people happier and better leaders, not to mention better family members and citizens of the community.

Make Your World Bigger

The first suggestion was to make your world smaller. The second suggestion, to make your world bigger, might seem, on the face of the language, to be the exact opposite. It isn't. It's actually a continuation of that third point above. The larger benefit of affluence is influence. Tragically, many turn their influence in such a direction that it impacts their small, little world. Philanthropists have provided resources, solutions, culture, and institutions that have blessed multiple generations. For those who've enjoyed individual success, there's no better response to that success than investing in a bigger world. Consider philanthropic endeavors that are larger than your world, your industry, and your direct field of influence.

Warren Buffett demonstrated incredible courage by choosing to channel his "bigger world" living through the foundation established by Bill and Melinda Gates. Here was one of the most successful investors of the twentieth century. He has plenty of money to start his own foundation. Yet Buffett decided to pool his money with others in an effort to solve the biggest problems people face. What are your plans to make your world bigger and better? I've often heard members of the older generation encourage the young to "leave the world a better place than you found it." If you've enjoyed success in the world, how can you repay that success?

CONCLUSION

In an interview about his life, Steve Jobs said, "Bottom line is, I didn't return to Apple to make a fortune. I've been very lucky in my life and already have one. When I was twenty-five, my net worth was $100 million or so. I decided then that I wasn't going to let it ruin my life. There's no way you could ever spend it all, and I don't view wealth as something that validates my intelligence."*

Jobs found a way to counteract the effect of money, and the world is better for it. If you've never really had large amounts of money, and suddenly you do, you can live beyond your means. Respect for frugality erodes, and you end up spending more than you have coming in. You neglect saving for the future and spend with the false belief that more money will always be there. You stop focusing enough on the practices, habits, and discipline that generated the wealth in the first place. Do not be fooled; money does change things. Will you own, or will you be owned? Win that war by making your world smaller. Win that war by making your world bigger. Make a personal commitment to live beneath your means while also having respect for generosity.

---

* Steve Jobs, "Apple's One-Dollar-a-Year Man," CNNMoney, CNN website, last modified January 24, 2000, http://money.cnn.com/magazines/fortune/fortune_archive/2000/01/24/272277/.

FROM THE WORLD OF EXPERIENCE

In my world as a consultant and advisor, I've seen people respond well to financial success, and I've seen other people respond poorly. Two clients, in particular, came from the same industry. They were both in insurance and financial services; they'd both started their own business and were self-declared entrepreneurs. That's where their stories diverge, though.

One entrepreneur—let's call her Sharon—took her success as a green light to change her lifestyle. As revenues from her business expanded rapidly, she decided she needed to interject a lot more capital in the expense side of things. She invested in sophisticated new technological infrastructure. She upgraded the facilities at her office, installing the nicest dark wood cabinets money could buy. She hired more employees. In short, as her revenues grew, her expenses grew to match them.

The second entrepreneur—let's call him Dave—did pretty much the opposite with his success. He was a smart guy and had set up his business the proper way. Soon, revenues started pouring in. But for years, Dave lived a life that was unchanged by the rapid growth in profitability. He didn't buy a new car. He didn't spend too much on upgrades around the office. He even kept his painful half-hour commute rather than upgrade with a downtown apartment. So what did he do with all that extra income? For a while, he drew out measured and reasonable distributions for himself. But he also invested appropriately in the business for longer-term, sustained growth. And those investments didn't come in the form of lavish new art on the walls. Dave invested in the things that would help grow his revenues even more! He hired consultants for his sales staff. He upgraded his incentive structures at the office to do a better job of retaining his top employees.

Twenty years later, who do you think was still in business? Who do you think enjoyed the most out of their money over time? The answer is fairly clear. Dave lived his life as if he'd known all along my three principles of "Make Your World Smaller." He saved his money for the long haul. He did not take short-term profits as an excuse to spend recklessly. And, eventually, that success led to his ability to make serious investments in the community through charitable philanthropy. Sharon enjoyed her money for a couple of years. But in a short time, she was forced to worry about it all over again. Meanwhile, Dave gets to spend his years working on causes closest to his heart.

I don't know why Dave answered the call the way he did or why Sharon answered it the way she did. It probably had something to do with their deeply ingrained values and perspectives of the world. But I don't think they were somehow indelibly wired to make the choices they did. With the right information, and a healthy dose of caution, you, too, can respond well to the wake-up call of money. You can choose to live simply and avoid excess. You can choose to save some of your money, armed with the knowledge that the world will eventually throw you a curveball. You may even be able to, after years of success, invest in the community to help solve the issues closest to your heart.

CHAPTER 4

UH-OH!
THE WAKE-UP CALL
OF FAILURE

*"Success is stumbling from failure to
failure with no loss of enthusiasm."*
—WINSTON CHURCHILL

*"I have heard there are troubles of more than one kind.
Some come from ahead and some come from behind.
But I've bought a big bat. I'm all ready you see.
Now my troubles are going to have troubles with me!"*
—DR. SEUSS

LEFT-HANDED PITCHERS WHO throw 97 miles per hour and can mix in a sharp curveball and stealthy changeup for a strike are usually going to find some level of success in pro baseball. Rick Ankiel was one of those pitchers. He was drafted out of high school, and within three years he was considered the very best minor-league prospect in all of baseball. When he was called up to play for the St. Louis Cardinals, he made thirty starts for a playoff team. He qualified for the earned-run average (ERA) title and struck out, on average, more than a batter an inning. His manager trusted him enough to send him to the mound for Game 1 of the National League playoffs against the Atlanta Braves. Rick Ankiel was very, very good. There was absolutely no reason to think that he'd have anything less than a long and productive career pitching.

In that Game 1 in early October, his first major-league playoff game, the wheels came off for this young prodigy. He breezed through the first couple of innings easily. After all, he had devastating pitches that flummoxed the poor batters. He'd succeeded because of his skills, and those skills were on full display. But in the third inning, things changed suddenly and terribly.

Ankiel walked four batters. He threw five wild pitches. If you're a baseball fan, you know that sometimes wild pitches aren't *totally* the pitcher's fault. Sometimes they are just reflections of an aggressive strategy. These weren't those types of wild pitches. The locations were not even close. A couple of pitches seemed to leap from Ankiel's hand directly into the backstop, leaving the catcher a mere observer in some odd unraveling of human talent. Those pitches that didn't fly into the backstop instead found the grass, failing to make it anywhere near the plate. Ankiel was pulled without getting out of the inning, and he headed to the dugout as mystified as everyone in the stadium.

The Cardinals won in spite of Ankiel getting pulled in the third inning. In fact, they won the playoff series. That fact is important for our story because it meant Ankiel got an opportunity at redemption. Ankiel's next appearance came against the Mets. This game went even worse than the previous one. He threw twenty pitches in the first inning. His catcher couldn't get close enough to five of them to even put a mitt on the ball. To put that in some perspective for non-baseball people, the American League average for wild pitches in nine innings in 2013 was 0.37.* In other words, most successful pitchers suffer a wild pitch once every four or five games. Ankiel had thrown five in one inning. He was beyond wild. To the outside observer, why he was on the mound in the first place would have been a mystery.

The next year, Ankiel's struggles continued in the pros before he was eventually sent back to the minor leagues to try to work out his control issues. This can't-miss prospect, who'd just months earlier been one of the best young talents in all of baseball, didn't pitch again in the majors for three years. In minor league ballparks throughout Middle America and the Northeast, Ankiel vacillated between good games and terrible ones. The glimpses of control didn't help matters. What pro teams look for in pitchers, in addition to skills, is the capacity to replicate certain moves consistently. During the course of weeks and months, Ankiel just could not get it together. He'd made it to the mountaintop in pro baseball. He'd pitched a Game 1 in the playoffs. He was a can't-miss prospect. And now, he couldn't throw the ball across the plate. If that isn't failure, I don't know what is.

Ankiel was not the first person to struggle with "the yips" (a sudden, unexplained loss of previous skills), nor are such examples limited to baseball. Pitcher Steve Blass of the Pittsburgh Pirates had the same issue and went from All-Star seasons to early retirement. Chuck Knoblauch, once one of the game's best second basemen, suddenly lost the ability to make the short throw to first base, perhaps the easiest throw in all of baseball. He was moved to the outfield for a while and then taken out of the defensive rotation altogether. Dale Murphy was a star catching prospect for the Braves until he lost the ability to throw the ball back to

---

* Edward Thoma, "Catchers and Wild Pitches," Baseball Outsider blog, last modified September 23, 2013, http://fpbaseballoutsider.blogspot.com/2013/09/catchers-and-wild-pitches.html.

the pitcher. Golfers have gone from zoned in to unable to make a one-foot putt. The yips often struck these people during the highest of stakes, on the eighteenth green or in the playoffs. These athletes offer a graphic and altogether extravagant depiction of failure. How did they respond?

This chapter talks about the power that failure can exert in our lives. It can be the most powerful motivational tool in the world, if you know how to leverage it. I address some of the different types of failure, then list some of the ways in which failure can be a wake-up call and the right ways to approach it. For that last bit, Ankiel's story will be our guide.

FAILURE HAPPENS TO SUCCESSFUL PEOPLE

The notion that failure can be a good thing is hardly limited to sports. Many people are familiar with the list of Abraham Lincoln's failures on his way to fulfilling the mission of ending slavery and preserving the union. It's so familiar, though, that it merits repeating. Before winning his only campaign to be president of the United States, Lincoln was defeated six times in elections for either the State House of Representatives in Illinois and for the US Congress. In what must have been the most stinging defeats, he twice lost reelection campaigns after completing successful terms in office. Outside of the political sphere, Mr. Lincoln oversaw the failure of two businesses, experienced the death of a girlfriend and child, and had a nervous breakdown at age twenty-seven. There is absolutely nothing in his résumé that would have remotely qualified him for the highest office in the land.

The failure of prominent figures in American history didn't start with Honest Abe. In 1492, Christopher Columbus sailed the ocean blue in a mission financed by Spain. He was charged with opening up trade routes to China. About five weeks after setting sail for the

"Far East," the Niña, Pinta, and Santa Maria reached a tiny island that is a part of modern-day Bahamas. The explorers darted around the islands east of America, eventually reaching the island of Cuba. It was there where the Europeans encountered tobacco and took up the habit.

The most important discovery of the fifteenth century was a series of failures. Columbus lost the largest of the three ships entrusted to him, and he failed at his ultimate goal. He never did locate that lucrative trade route to China. Most embarrassing in hindsight, in Columbus's own mind, is that he never believed he had discovered a new land. He never fully contemplated the magnitude of his discovery. The greatest economic reward from his exploration would be slavery and tobacco, arguably the bane of the American experience in the years that followed. In a stinging rebuke to what Columbus had actually done, Queen Isabella chose not to continue exploration of the New World.

THE CASE OF MJ—FAILURE IS GOOD

Michael Jordan is recognized as one of the greatest basketball players of all time. Between the years of 1982 and 1998, Jordan won six NBA championships, one NCAA title, five MVP awards, and two Olympic gold medals. He made countless last-second, game-winning shots. He was a nightly highlight reel. He maintained that status with a brash attitude and fearlessness against his opponents. For those who started watching Jordan in his later years, it would've been difficult to imagine him ever struggling or failing to succeed. Yet, when media members asked Jordan the source of his motivation, he never failed to mention the impact that failing early in life had on him. He lost countless games of basketball in his backyard to his older brother, Larry. But the most significant failure has also become one of the most well-known. Jordan was in his sophomore year in high school at the time. He was invited to try out for the varsity basketball team with his brother. His skill made an impression, but at 5'11", his relatively short stature prompted the coach to leave his name off the list. Michael Jordan, the greatest basketball player the world has ever known, didn't make his high-school basketball team!

If you can remember your middle-school or high-school days, you probably also remember the way those lists are posted publicly for all to see. How difficult that moment is for anyone, to register internally that they've failed to make the cut at the same time peers learn of their own successes. The day the varsity team was announced, Michael Jordan read and reread the list of those who made the cut. Initially, he experienced disbelief, assuming a mistake was made. When he went to inquire, the coach's choice was confirmed. Jordan would indeed spend the year playing on the junior-varsity team. First, the young man wept. But his response did not end with weeping.

Jordan became a maniacal worker. This event led to his implementing a new regimen of working out, practicing, and organizing his life around the vision of making the list the next year. He spent more time in the gym working on his footwork. He shot more practice free throws. The next year, he made the cut. But the impact of that failure lasted far longer. Jordan once said, "Whenever I achieve some success but feel so tired, I often come to think to give up and leave everything. But then I close my eyes and see again that list that didn't include my name. Usually by doing that, my spirit is revived." In his Hall of Fame speech years later, Jordan recounted each and every slight that had motivated him over the years. He sounded almost monomaniacal. But certainly no one would dispute the impact of that perspective.

Takeaways—What to Do with All This Failure?

These stories demonstrate a couple of universal truths. The first is that failure can be a powerful motivational tool. For years after he'd achieved great success, Michael Jordan looked back to that moment of pain as a reason to work just a bit harder, to run just a bit longer or faster, to shoot one hundred more free throws. On the opposite side of the spectrum, Abraham Lincoln's failures taught him humility and intentionality that were essential character traits in navigating the excruciating demands of a civil war. When Lincoln freed the slaves via the Emancipation Proclamation, he didn't do it as a man who'd known nothing but successes. He did it as a man of empathy, a man who had experienced life's hardships and could understand the plight of others.

I've always thought that the stories of Michael Jordan and Christopher Columbus also show the importance of having some perspective. Short-term setbacks often have very little to do with long-term consequences. We are often too focused on the immediate to contemplate the broad fully; we lose sight of the forest for the trees. Also, our naïve fascination with short-term results often focuses on a rather unimportant result far more than it does on the process by which that result was reached.

I've sometimes heard friends in the teaching world argue that this happens all the time in middle school. Parents get obsessed with letter grades and the numerical value placed on a particular quiz or test. In the process, those parents totally lose track of what actually matters: long-term learning habits and mastery of the skills that will help their kid in the future. Who cares what you make in seventh-grade pre-algebra? Who even remembers what grades they made back then? I don't. But I know that some of the work habits I was forced to adopt are still with me. I know that the lessons

I learned from struggling on smaller assignments taught me how to study more effectively. I know that, by working diligently for the grade, I gained comprehension skills and the ability to make connections. *What matters is the process.* Far too many potential leaders sit on the sidelines, held hostage by their fear of failure. If we fully understand that failure is not only essential to success and that it often is the *source* of success, we might be better prepared to act.

TYPES OF FAILURE

The way you respond to failure ultimately will be based on what kind of failures you've experienced. A kid who fails a math quiz after failing to study isn't going to do better by wanting it more. A middle manager who fails to connect with his employees is not going to do better just by trying harder. Sometimes we have to change our approach in a fundamental way. We have to tailor our response and our efforts to achieve a different result, to the nature of the problem that prevented success in the first place. Other times, we just need to exert a bit more effort. Let's look briefly at some "types of failure" to gain more clarity about the best responses.

Failure of Relationships

The fundamental challenge of leadership is in establishing and maintaining successful relationships. The ability to forge trust in a relationship is essential to long-term effectiveness. If you take a quick survey of the stakeholders most essential to your success as a leader (subordinates, staff, vendors, clients, colleagues) and the results reveal doubts about choices you're making, you need to listen to that wake-up call. Every business book and web resource has its own list of leadership characteristics essential for success. All of those lists involve some dimension of success in interactions with other people. Leaders need to be good at both upward and downward relationships. Good leaders need trusted advisors. If they run a nonprofit, they need positive dynamics with their board. They also need employees to whom they can delegate responsibility for essential tasks. They need to convey to get others on track with the vision and mission of the organization and satisfy their employees' search for validation and meaning at work. If you are a supervisor, ask yourself these questions:

1. Are my relationships with subordinates safe for them?

2. Do I have successful partnerships with peers?

3. How productive are my relationships with mentors?

4. Am I failing or succeeding at the relationships in my life?

Failure of Effort

During the course of your life, ideas and opportunities sometimes come along. When they do, for a variety of reasons, you may choose to play it safe and take no action. These failures are a dominant theme in the stories of people whose lives have been marred with regret. If you listen long enough to the tales told by earlier generations, you will find that a lot more regret is associated with the things they did *not* do than what they *did* do. They often wish they'd gone on that crazy trip to Europe or asked that pretty girl out. Sometimes, they wish they'd had the courage to take that risky job offer when they were young or tried to walk-on in a college sport. Rarely do they regret doing something wild and crazy twenty years ago, and not just because they have better stories as a result of that crazy thing! Ask yourself the following questions as you consider whether or not your failures are related to a lack of effort:

1. What in my story reflects a choice not to pursue something risky?

2. Why did I let the opportunity pass me by?

3. What idea was left unexplored?

As you reflect on these questions, do you hear an alarm going off, prompting you to wake up? Maybe there is some unexplored business initiative you've been putting off for too long. Maybe your career arc has stagnated and you need to make a change. Don't settle. And don't fall prey to the failure of effort. In many cases, it isn't too late to pursue old dreams. In any case, it's always the right time to start pursuing new ones.

Failure of Ambition

In Arthur Miller's play *Death of a Salesman*, at the graveside of main character Willy Loman, one of the mourners comments, "He had all the wrong dreams." In that play, Willy Loman is motivated primarily by "dreams" of material success. It's one of the overarching messages of the play—that the American dream also has elements of greed. And Miller certainly is ambivalent about the ethical components of struggling for a lifetime for those sorts of material rewards. If he were to phrase it, he might even go so far as to call his opinions critical.

One of the most painful things to observe is the waste of time, talent, and resources on a worthless pursuit. It's far better to fail because you've pursued the wrong objective than it is to succeed in an empty pursuit. I once heard someone say that if you haven't failed some, your dreams aren't big enough. We need to have big dreams like Willy Loman did, but we also have to make sure that they are the right kind of dreams. Daniel Pink's *Drive*, which I'll come back to again and again, argues that the best way to motivate people is to give them a sense of "purpose." Research shows that "purpose" and "meaning" are much more effective long-term motivational tools than money. As you think about the failures you've encountered in your own history, I'd encourage you to think of two big questions:

1. What are my ambitions?

   • What are they, really? What is the driving source of them, the underlying motivation?

2. In short, are they for material things or something deeper?

Either way, recognizing that your ambitions have been misguided can be a profound wake-up call. An effective leader practices a high level of self-awareness. Along the way, he or she constantly asks the question, "Are my pursuits admirable?" A Buddhist spoke on the "Noble Eightfold Path" called "Right Livelihood." Way back in the 400s BCE, the Buddha was arguing that your occupation ought to be—if you are to be a spiritually healthy individual—good for the world and the creatures in it. But thinking about whether or not that's the case takes a great deal of self-awareness and reflective analysis. That sort of thing doesn't come naturally to many people. In fact, it can be downright hard.

In my career, when I've spoken to professionals, I've found two characteristics that are most common among highly successful individuals. (By successful, I mean a combination of material success and skill at life in general. They enjoy market share or material well-being, but they also appreciate their success, are confident, and generally enjoy themselves.) Those two qualities are as follows:

1. **The ability to look at a diagram of information and quickly recognize what information is relevant and what is not**—The ability to judge relevance is consistent.

2. **Self-awareness**—The most successful leaders know how others perceive them. They don't always take that understanding and act fuzzy and sweet. They're just aware of when the act of being themselves is actually productive and when they need to tone it down.

The first trait is a bit less relevant to our argument here. When you're thinking about your own ambitions, think about how others perceive you as well. If you asked your assistant what your ambitions are, what would he or she say? What can you do to make those ambitions clear to others?

Failure of Time or Talent

Working with business leaders who attempt new initiatives, I have had, from time to time, to help them interpret what might have gone wrong. Failure of an idea, opportunity, or initiative often stems from not allowing enough time for those things to grow. We all need time to achieve additional or new work. A good rule of thumb in advocating change initiatives, which I found in the *Harvard Business Review* way back in 2005, is that employees shouldn't have to devote more than 10 percent of their time to them. This rule holds *unless, and only unless,* you're willing to take something off their plate as well.* This is part of the DICE

---

* Harold L. Sirkin, Perry Keenan, and Alan Jackson, "The Hard Side of Change Management," *Harvard Business Review* website, last modified October 2005, http://hbr.org/2005/10/the-hard-side-of-change-management.

framework, which gives recommendations about the duration of change initiatives, the level of expertise needed to drive them forward, and the commitment of top management to the goal. Too often, we have grand intentions for new things. But we don't allocate the time needed for those things to succeed, either structurally or intentionally.

That framework highlights the fact that you need both time and talent to achieve something. Malcolm Gladwell has written about the "10,000-hour rule" in his book *Outliers*. He highlights the Beatles, Bill Gates, and other successful entrepreneurs who achieved great success only after spending a great deal of time working on their goals. But recently, his rule has come under some attack. Critics have charged that *some people can put in those hours and still not achieve their goals*. Of course they can! You need some innate talent as well as a time commitment. NFL quarterback Peyton Manning puts in plenty of time in the film room. But he also has a pretty good genetic line for throwing a football. You can't do a lot about the talent issue other than be aware of your own limitations. But you can very much control that variable of time. Ask yourself: *Did I put in the 10,000 hours that greatness requires?* Even if you have the talent, you'll have to devote yourself to developing it.

If you put in the requisite time and it still didn't happen for you, you might have to ruminate a bit on whether or not you have the particular talent needed for success in this arena. Savvy entrepreneurs know when they ought to give up something that they don't do particularly well. Jim Collins talks in his book *Good to Great* about the hedgehog concept. This goes back to an older parable about a fox that spends all of its time trying to catch a hedgehog. The fox goes to great lengths to achieve this goal. He tracks the hedgehog, plans points of surprise, and scouts out the best locations for catching his nemesis. The hedgehog, meanwhile, does only one thing well: When he perceives trouble is near, he curls up in a ball that makes it impossible for the fox to harm him. The hedgehog, Collins argues, knows one thing. And he knows it exceedingly well. If you have failed at something, it might make sense to ask yourself: Is this something I can know/do exceedingly well? Or should I abandon this and try to do something I can do better or more naturally?

Failure of Character

This is the most terrible kind of failure, and it's probably the hardest one to rectify. It's sometimes said that character is *who you are when nobody is watching*. My grandmother used to tell me that you could tell who a man really is by how he treats people from whom he needs nothing. Everyone treats his or her boss, or someone from whom they need something, well. It's the people who treat others well who have real character. Sometimes, failure related to character is rooted in an inability to see your behaviors as others would see them. It's a failure of imaginative empathy. Richard Nixon, for example, argued for a long time that he was "not a crook." He reasoned this to be the case because, as president, he was above the law. Nixon was not a dumb man. He suffered, in this instance, a terrible lack of self-awareness.

Immanuel Kant, whose philosophy is one of the more popular foundations for ethics today, argued about the "categorical imperative." This concept meant that an action was good only if it would be appropriate for everyone to do it. Had Nixon viewed himself through Kant's lens, he would've seen just how "crooked" his actions were. He failed to do so for years and even grew angry about the ways in which he'd been wronged. An epiphany of sorts might have occurred during Nixon's interviews with David Frost. By that point, though, the damage to Nixon's public perception was done. Nixon didn't regain a bit of face until Bill Clinton, who also struggled with public perception issues, invited Nixon back into the fold.

One leader/client once shared with me, "Humiliation is a horrible way to learn humility." You're sure to be humiliated eventually if you suffer from failures of character. Ask yourself these questions:

1. What am I doing to nurture my character?

2. Am I, in reality, the kind of leader I want others to believe I am?

3. If I were an outside and objective observer, what would my perception of my daily activities be?

CONCLUSION

As you review the arenas of potential failure, do not be afraid to be truthful with yourself about who you really are. You can't begin to change things until you have a firm grasp on reality. A bold acknowledgment and confrontation of failure can serve as the platform from which you dive into a new level of success. Failure is never final. As you consider that truth, remember the "failure" of Columbus. This man didn't achieve his immediate objective. But, in retrospect, his objective was limited by what was known. What he discovered was far greater and more important for human history than a trade route. Much of the way we assess our life and leadership is done in snapshots, while in reality, we live in video footage. It's impossible to conclude the final outcome in one moment in time. A broader perspective allows us to answer the wake-up call and move forward with a heightened sense of curiosity. How can this temporary failure lead to an ultimate success? Moreover, how can you cultivate in yourself a tolerance for this longer view of what success is?

Implicit in our earlier discussion of Michael Jordan and Abe Lincoln is the message that quitting in the face of failure is the wrong choice. Let's look intentionally at a couple of famous responses to failure. Here, we'll talk about a few new people, but we'll also go back to our erratic Cardinals pitcher, Rick Ankiel.

In Chapter 3, I quoted Steve Jobs about his dismissal from Apple. What I didn't talk about is what he did when he was fired. Jobs was let go after clashing with Apple's board of directors in 1983. He was fired, in fact, by the very guy Jobs himself had appointed as CEO. Soon thereafter, Jobs sold all of his shares of Apple. He then set out to design a computer specifically aimed toward higher education and research at a company called *NeXT*. A few years later, he sold *NeXT* for $400 million. Not an insignificant chunk of change for a rebound gig! And, that was Jobs's lesser achievement. He also started a digital film company and got to work on a minor animated film called *Toy Story*. By the time he was done with Pixar, Jobs sold his shares in the company for $1 billion. (That "b" is correct!)

Failure can be a wake-up call or quicksand in which you spend the next years of your life trapped. Confronted with his choice, Jobs treated his initial failure as a wake-up call. He didn't get mired in the details of his dismissal. He changed without totally reinventing himself. He learned from his mistakes. But he also waited for other people to learn from theirs! He never let go of Apple as an option to which he would return. But he was patient. Jobs also doubled down on his skills and visionary capacity. He didn't change industries. He didn't back down and take a less-ambitious gig. Instead, he took the skills and talents that made him who he was at Apple and pumped those things into new roles. Here, we can turn back to our story of Rick Ankiel. When it comes to baseball players with the yips, Ankiel is actually an odd version of a success story. The guy for whom the control problem, called "Steve Blass Disease," is named— former Pirates pitcher Blass—had to retire two years into his case with the yips. Ankiel took a slightly different approach.

Ankiel approached the problem from a capacity-based perspective. He asked himself, "What qualities got me here? What can I still do? What is true about me that led me to even have this chance to fail so spectacularly? I was in the pros, after all. How did I get there in the first place?" His interpretation of events was not, "I stink." It was, "I was willing to put in the hours before that no one else was willing to put in. Maybe I just need to redirect and use the talents I've been given." So he asked the Cardinals if he could start over as an outfielder. It helped that Ankiel had been, for a pitcher, a pretty good hitter in the first place. He'd always been an outstanding athlete, and for some reason, his throwing arm worked accurately from the outfield position, even though it had failed him from the mound. After working at it for a couple of years, Ankiel once again made it back to the major leagues. This time, he did so as an outfielder. He wasn't a Rookie of the Year candidate or an All-Star. But he had a successful career as a major league player at his *second* position.

QUESTIONS FOR THOUGHT

Two of the keys to overcoming failure are self-awareness and the ability to put failure in the right context. Ask yourself these questions:

1. Do I know, when I fail, why things didn't work?

2. Am I thinking big picture or small?

3. What kind of failure was this? What kind of response is merited?

4. Have I failed enough in my life? (Are my ambitions ambitious enough?)

President Franklin D. Roosevelt famously said, "We have nothing to fear but fear itself." Failure is not something to fear. It's an opportunity for growth. Approach your troubles the way Dr. Seuss encourages us at the beginning of the chapter. Find your own "big bat" and make sure that your troubles have trouble with you. Think of failure as a stepping stone to the next great adventure. It can teach you powerful lessons if you let it. Will you answer the wake-up call of failure?

CHAPTER 5

OH, NO!
THE WAKE-UP CALL
OF LOSS

For certain is death for the born
And certain is birth for the dead;
Therefore over the inevitable
Thou shouldst not grieve.
—THE BHAGAVAD GITA

Don't cry because it's over.
Smile because it happened.
—DR. SEUSS

THE FIRST QUOTE above is from the famous Hindu text, the one that Gandhi read every morning in his daily devotionals. It's indeed provocative. While I might not agree with the notion that grief is unnecessary because mortality is inevitable, this chapter is about the wake-up call of loss. This wake-up call often comes as a dark period in people's lives. Even if you make it through loss without much darkness, this type of failure is still less exciting than some of the others we've discussed. Yet it will happen regardless of how much we deny its inevitability. But the type of loss the Gita quote above addresses is only a start to the types of loss I address in this chapter. Along the way, I'll echo the quote from Dr. Seuss above about viewing loss as an event to prompt positive memories. I'll also give some ways to walk through loss to get to the other side.

Frequently in life, people view the concept of loss and grief too narrowly. We are all acquainted with, and patient toward, people grieving the loss of a loved one. That form of loss is perhaps the most terrible and difficult to bear. But there are numerous common events that we perceive as losses. To start thinking about this variety, let's take a look at the following scenarios. I'm confident that at least one of these situations is familiar to you.

Jan's Story

Jan began mapping her future as soon as she sat in her freshman English class in high school. With rigor and discipline, she was confident she would graduate in the top 5 percent of her class and go to the school of her choice. You can imagine the sense of accomplishment she felt when she was accepted to Columbia University and was on the fast track to a career in journalism. Following a successful Ivy League experience, Jan was recruited and hired by *The New York Times*. With the same kind of focus she displayed from the beginning of her high-school experience, Jan climbed the journalistic ladder with ease. Upon returning to her ten-year high school reunion, she could wow old friends with the people she interviewed and the stories she broke. But, as Jan enjoyed milestone after milestone, the entire industry started to shift beneath her feet. With the rise of online media and the turn away from investigative journalism, the skills and relationships Jan built over time became less relevant. Story assignments slowed down, and eventually Jan lost her job due to a massive downsizing in an ailing industry. This is a loss that must be grieved.

Marcus's Story

Marcus started a small engineering firm with some of his colleagues from his days with a defense contractor. The big idea that birthed their dream was the development of a new technology that would have widespread usage in the marketplace. Marcus was able to secure funding with the help of venture capital, contingent on securing a patent on the new technology. Unknown to Marcus and this start-up firm, a group of competitors beat them to the punch, and the patent was quashed. They lost the capital, they lost the firm, and tragically, they lost their friendship. This is a loss that must be grieved.

Olivia's Story

Olivia was an amazing organizational genius. With the talent of a Las Vegas juggler, she could keep her children's schedule, her business obligations, and her friendships all moving fluidly without dropping anything. Olivia began to see some light at the end of the tunnel as her children approached marriage and college graduation. Her skill was about to pay off when she was approached by a larger company to buy her business. After years of balancing the demands of family and business, she could completely stack the deck in favor of family. As the plans for the sale of the business were taking shape, Olivia was making plans for scaling back and getting more involved in her charitable work. All of that excitement evaporated when she was diagnosed with late-stage pancreatic cancer. All of the juggling, all of that work, now paled in the possibility that she could die. This is a loss that must be grieved.

Frank's Story

Frank had always been a visionary. He'd seen holes in the market where others hadn't, and he'd invented and patented several products that made his chosen industry more efficient. One idea led to another, until finally he was a respected ideas man in his field. Twenty years into his career, things were rolling. Then, one day, he went to make a pitch and was asked things he had yet to fully consider. A younger businessman swept in behind him and stole the client, and Frank was left wondering if he still had it. The loss of his youth was something he had to grieve.

These stories are not shared in succession to pull at your heartstrings like a Budweiser commercial—those adorable big-footed horses and their clumsy colts!—during the Super Bowl. Instead, these stories are meant to illustrate the various types of loss we encounter during the course of our leadership. These types of losses plague everyone: followers, leaders, and middle management. The implications of those tragedies can be magnified, though, when they happen to a leader. When a loss permanently sidelines a leader, other people and organizations in general suffer. First, let's categorize the types of loss entrepreneurs will (almost inevitably) face in the course of their careers.

1. **Loss of life**—When you lose significant people in your life—a parent through death, a close friend because of a disagreement, or a spouse in divorce—the grief can be overwhelming.

2. **Loss of money, capital, or profit margin**—This can be sudden or a slow and steady decline. It can happen because of market changes or with the rise of a competitor.

3. **Loss of health**—As we age, our energy levels become diminished. We were able to do things when we were younger that we can't do now. At some point in our lives, we realize that an increase in age is directly correlated to a decrease in youth and energy.

4. **Loss of vision**—A loss of passion and a corresponding rise of cynicism relate to the loss of vision we once had as a leader.

It's not easy to muster the courage to move forward when you lose your best customer. It's not easy to recover momentum when you lose out on a great opportunity in an exciting new market. It's not easy to keep your pace when you start to struggle with nagging health problems. It's not easy to remember your purpose for leading and growing when you lose someone you love. It's not easy to pick yourself up and try again when you lose the cash flow and income level to which you've grown accustomed. Because it's not easy, it's imperative that we learn about loss and discover productive ways to incorporate it into our leadership life.

Let's look at a couple examples of loss and corresponding responses as a means of searching for the "right" steps to take.

Two Different Responses to Loss

1. Personal/Family

In January 2012, my father passed away as suddenly as an eighty-four-year-old can pass away. He'd been in good health, and aside from being a bit on the older side, his death came as some surprise to all of his family. His death, and the way I responded to it, offers one response to the wake-up call of loss. It isn't the only way, but it worked for me.

Dad and I had always had a fairly positive relationship, despite the fact that we were, in many ways, cut from different sorts of cloth. He was a CPA, a corporate accountant. From the days of my childhood, he worked diligently. He was less fearful than he was conservative and cautious. Inevitably, when I told him of my entrepreneurial ideas, he encouraged caution in addition to exercising it. "You've got a wife and kids," he'd say. "Where are you going to get health insurance?" he returned to again and again. I didn't begrudge Dad these questions. They were good ones to ask. Any entrepreneur knows that a steady dose of caution is generally helpful. But I hung my shingle anyway. And, by the time Dad passed away, I'd reached a level of success that both comforted and shocked him.

As fate would have it, his death came the day before one of the more important days in my professional career. I was set to deliver a strategic presentation to a group of entrepreneurs. We'd been working toward this conference for a while. We'd drummed up attendees and had charted the course of content. Our aspiring business hinged in some ways on success, which hopefully would yield future clients and business.

So I had a choice to make: rush home to be with my family in grief or stick around to finish things up with this major event and then fly home. As I worked through the day with those entrepreneurs, I was hit by a reality: In showing up at work that day, I was modeling one of the things Dad modeled to me. We had our different perspectives about what level of work was suitable for a family man. He worried about the risks I was taking for myself. But some of his essential principles got through to me anyway. Foremost among those lessons was the importance of simply showing up. Follow through. Be responsible. I felt that my sense of responsibility for this business came from Dad's efforts to instill it in me long ago.

And, when I chose to stick around and do the training, it was in some ways a means of harnessing my grief for something positive.

2. Career/Reputation

In April 2012, during the first playoff game of the Chicago Bulls' postseason hunt for a title, Derrick Rose, NBA superstar and the league's Most Valuable Player from the previous season, suffered a season-ending knee injury. This injury ended the Bulls' title hopes for that year. Sports journalists proffered theories about the cause of the injury. They lambasted the Bulls coach for having left in his star player late in a game that was already decided. They worried that the season was now too long and that systemic changes in league schedules were necessary. Who could've known that in the spring of 2012, the controversy was just beginning?

For the entirety of the next season, the city of Chicago and NBA fans waited eagerly for the return of their great point guard. Adidas put out an emotionally evocative ad that depicted Rose as a modern champion working through every obstacle to return and reclaim his status. Doctors first talked glowingly of his efforts to rehab the knee, then officially cleared him to play a couple of weeks before playoffs began at the end of the 2013 season. Prognosticators wondered if Rose might push the Bulls back into contention. If they could only hold out long enough for him to play back into shape, the Bulls would be a dangerous team.

Yet, as his teammates played valiantly and won nail-biter after nail-biter, Rose stayed on the bench in street clothes. While doctors insisted he was fine, Rose quietly and unceremoniously maintained that the knee wasn't ready. He'd participated in practices, but he still felt unprepared for the speed of an NBA game. After the Bulls surprisingly won their first playoff round, the debate intensified. Surely Rose would come back now! Surely he would valiantly return in some storybook ending. He didn't. The one person who might've swung a playoff series against LeBron James and the Miami Heat sat on the sidelines. As he did so, Rose was criticized for a lack of heart and passion. His reputation had previously been that of a diligent worker; now fans questioned his commitment to his team. The ownership of the team publicly supported their superstar's choice, but internal murmuring intensified.

This story illustrates, on the one hand, that there's certainly more than one type of *knowing*. Rose *knew* how much a game took out of his body. He *knew* where he needed to be to compete. So a doctor's conclusions, based on pictures from a giant magnet, certainly don't merit absolute and total faith. Rose's example, and the criticism he endured for his refusal to play in the 2013 playoffs, also offer an interesting counter to the biographical anecdote I shared earlier. He most certainly suffered a loss. He was injured during the most critical time in the season, and during the peak of his prime. Professional athletes usually don't get more than fifteen years of excellence. Rose lost one of those precious years in a fluke accident. Had he played well in those playoffs, he would've built on his legacy. He would've further cemented his status as one of the best players in the game. Instead, he waited. As he did so, what was his grieving like?

It couldn't have been easy for him to watch his teammates go out and battle while he sat idly by. It would've been tempting for him to rejoin them triumphantly. Yet he waited. Rose stands as the alternative to my personal approach following the loss of my father. He *knew* what he needed to do to recover. He trusted his choice and stood by it. The metaphor here is physical, but it was also emotional and mental. He allowed himself time to rebound. He went through the steps he thought were necessary. Reports coming out of the Chicago locker room preceding the start of the 2012 season were that Rose's vertical jump had improved by five inches. Prior to his ACL injury, he was soaring about 37 inches off the ground. Post-injury, he was purportedly at 42 inches. He'd certainly be rusty, but that metric suggested that he was coming back from his injury stronger than ever. His courage in sticking to that choice was certainly remarkable. His approach to loss was to fully accept it, to return from it methodically and intentionally, to stare at loss dead in the face, and to walk back from it with purpose.

Unfortunately, we'll now see what Rose chose to do in almost exactly the same scenario. After waiting for a season and a half to return, Rose tore the ACL in his opposite knee just fifteen games into the 2013 season. Will he make the same choices in dealing with this loss as he did the last time? Will he have learned from that experience and act differently? Time will tell. By the time you are reading this book, you might know from having seen those choices in action. What do you think of them?

FIVE STAGES—THE STANDARD MODEL

The two stories at the beginning of this chapter seem so different. What links them? What links our method of grieving to that of others? The most popular conception of grief—the one cited in books and websites and by every armchair psychiatrist—comes from the work of Elisabeth Kübler-Ross. She came up with the "five stages of grief," which she termed as follows:

1. **Denial**—"I'll be fine; surely this can't be happening."

2. **Anger**—"Why did this have to happen? This isn't fair. Who is to blame?!"

3. **Bargaining**—"I'll do anything for a few more years of health. I'll pay whatever it takes."

4. **Depression**—"I'm too sad to bother with anything. Who cares?"

5. **Acceptance**—"It's going to be OK. I can't fight it any longer. I may as well prepare for the inevitable."

The following chart describes these five stages further.

FIVE STAGES OF GRIEF

		DENIAL	BARGAINING	ANGER	DEPRESSION	ACCEPTANCE
		Ignore the wake-up call.	Hit the snooze button.	Throw the alarm clock across the room.	Interpret the wake-up call in a counter-productive way.	Effectively re-interpret the wake-up call!
TYPE OF LOSS	**Life**	This did not happen	If I work harder and am successful this will not hurt.	This should not have happened.	Because this happened why move forward?	Things will never be the same, but they can be good.
	Money	I can spend/save my way forward.	Maybe I should try this…	I was wronged!	I lost my one and only chance.	I did it before, I can do it again.
	Health	I can still do this.	I will get better when…	Why did this happen to me?	This can't be done because…	We can't get it done this way…
	Vision	Nothing has changed.	Can I continue doing what I am doing now, if…	The world should not have changed. We are right.	The future is lost.	I see a new image of a better future.

A couple of disclaimers are necessary when it comes to these stages. Kübler–Ross never intended them to be a rigid or linear framework, a model into which all forms of grief fit nicely and neatly. She once said that they "were never meant to help tuck messy emotions into neat packages. They are responses to loss that many people have, but *there is not a typical response to loss, as there is no typical loss.* Our grieving is as individual as our lives."*

To go back to my personal example, when Dad died, I made a few choices about what to do with the days immediately after. And I made a choice that I still think was the correct one. But when that conference was over, I wandered through some of Kübler–Ross's stages. I felt angry. I denied that the world had fundamentally shifted. I struggled some days more than others. And it certainly impacted my work in ways I couldn't even perceive.

I believe that these stages of grief can manifest in entrepreneurs in particular ways. In the life of a business leader or an innovator, grief can have some trademark attributes that fit Kübler–Ross's stages. Let's take a look at each of them in our particular context:

1. **Denial**—It can be tempting for entrepreneurs to believe, when a terrible thing happens in their personal lives, that, however sad they might be, "It won't affect my business." Leaders can be overly confident in their ability to compartmentalize. When leaders compartmentalize, though, often they just procrastinate their grieving process, which in the long term will affect them much more virulently. Telling yourself that you are not affected certainly does not mean that what you are telling yourself is true.

2. **Bargaining**—The word I would use for bargaining is "integration." When entrepreneurs lose some dimension of their life, they often tend to believe that they've "worked too hard" or put one component of their life

---

* "Coping with Grief and Loss," HelpGuide.org website, http://www.helpguide. org/mental/grief_loss.htm.

above others. One of the common misunderstandings in the business world is around the idea of "life balance." The misconception holds that there's some proper ratio of business to personal, some healthy dynamic toward which the conscientious leader will strive. This conception holds that business isn't personal, and vice versa. Proponents of this view would argue that when you go home, you need to make sure you unplug your phone and "turn work off." What you really need to do is to integrate your business in such a way that you can invest in the future and incorporate your personal and professional needs. Ask yourself, "How do I incorporate my hobbies into my professional life? How do I integrate strategic relationships into my personal life?" What you do should be a reflection of who you are. Work you do should be aligned with values you possess. The old separation of personal life and business life should be a way of the past. If you need to cut work off when you get home, you are in the wrong sector of business!

3. **Anger**—In the life of an entrepreneur, when faced with one of the categories of loss we started out discussing, anger can often manifest as resentment and resignation. You might become bitter about the impact of the business on your personal life or about the perceived ways in which business kept you from keeping in personal contact frequently enough. You might grow to resent your work, get angry at work. Alternatively, anger can lead to resignation. You can be tempted to resign yourself to the ever-powerful influence of your business world over all components of your life. You may cede that this entrepreneurial venture is going to be an all-

encompassing process. It's hard to lead something that you resent or have resigned yourself to. Anger in the face of loss rarely helps a leader do her or his job.

4. **Depression**—For an entrepreneur, everything depends on purpose and drive. The great inventors throughout human history have always felt motivated by some broader sense of a better future. They wake up every day thinking about the possible. What blow could be worse, then, in the face of loss than to lose your purpose? Often, loss can lead entrepreneurs to do just that. They might sink into a depression from which the vision of a better future and the dreams of the possible seem distant and unattainable. To me, this is the saddest and toughest form of grief an entrepreneur can face.

5. **Acceptance**—In Kübler–Ross's "stages" model, the notion of acceptance is essentially what others might term "coming out on the other side." Acceptance is the beginning of turning the page. At dangerous times, and similar to the depression stage described above, sometimes acceptance can lead to apathy and existential doubt in the life of an entrepreneur, who might ask himself, "What is the point?" The more ideal version of acceptance, I'd argue, is for that same person to ask these questions as he's grieving: "How do I use this to be better at what I do? What lessons did I learn from this person? How did this person or this event impact me, and how can I leverage that?"

LOOKING FORWARD THROUGH LOSS

When I think back on my response to Dad's death, that event wasn't a devastating or debilitating thing. I interpreted it in a way that enabled me to function at a high level. I used the loss to reflect on all the things I'd gained in a lifetime of learning from my father. I took his lessons to heart even when it was difficult to do so, and I feel like I ended up a bit closer to the man he always pushed me to be. I grieved in a way that was respectful of Dad's legacy and that brought me closer to him.

Now I know that all grief is different and that everyone grieves in his or her own way. It would be quite a different thing to face the loss of a child than to face the loss of a parent who'd lived a long and productive life. I'm not recommending that everyone go back to work the day after a loved one dies. This was just my own way of honoring my father. It felt right for me to get back to business. It made me feel more at peace and more purposeful. What I do recommend is that everyone try to come out of their grief—whenever they're ready—more at peace and more purposeful.

A SPECIAL BURDEN

A conversation I have with my clients on numerous occasions entails reminding them that they "get paid the big bucks because they are willing to carry a burden that others will not carry." The rationale behind that reminder is actually a bit more empathic than it might seem at first glance. Every leader understands that there's a persistent level of stress she carries. But few actually think much about the science behind that stress.

The science is scary and demands action. This heightened level of stress will activate prolonged periods of the brain, releasing a hormone known as cortisol into the bloodstream. Elevated levels of cortisol will cause high blood sugar, high blood pressure, and lower levels of white blood cells. This combination leaves the body physically vulnerable to cardiovascular disease and other chronic illness. Under normal circumstances, leaders are able to regulate this problem by exercising greater control over their calendar and engaging in activities that renew the mind and body. However, when we encounter what the brain considers "loss," the sympathetic nervous system might be engaged for a prolonged period of time and can override many of the efforts the body puts in place to regulate the volume of cortisol in the body. In other words, when we experience loss in any form, the systems the brain has in place to protect us begin to attack the body.

LEADERSHIP, GRIEF, AND STRESS

That problem is exacerbated by a central fact of leadership. We often operate in a culture that expects us to act as normal as possible in the face of instability. Moreover, as leaders, our job often involves creating stability and security for our teams. This dynamic often creates additional pressure for leaders to move through the grieving process at an accelerated clip and to pretend that all things are normal. Almost anyone can lead an organization when times are easy and business is booming. What separates genuine leaders from the fakes is how they cope during times of stress. One of the defining moments for every leader is how they deal with physical and psychological effects of loss. If you're a leader struggling with meaning, power, and purpose, it could be connected to not navigating loss in a way that's productive. Consider some of the following suggestions as a way to hear and respond to your wake-up call.

Grieving

So what to do? First, do not buy into the myth that deaths are the only events that warrant grieving. The brain has the capacity to interpret all change as a loss equal to death. Do you find yourself struggling with motivation at times? Is the effectiveness of your leadership hampered by bouts of cynicism? When a big decision is needed and a bold move warranted, do you find yourself to be uncharacteristically cautious or reluctant to act? Do you lack the energy to try again? These questions could help you diagnose the possibility that you might not have fully grieved an earlier loss. I consider grieving to be, as weird as this might sound, a necessary business strategy. Everything within a successful entrepreneur is about *go*, and everything about grieving is about *slow*. Think of grief as a necessary and unavoidable business reality. Consider the following four steps to promote what I call productive grieving:

1. Diagnose the potential of an ungrieved loss.

2. Name the loss with specificity.

3. Describe the implications of the loss without avoiding the pain.

4. Be willing to mourn the loss.

Mourning

In the minds of many, there is little distinction between grieving and mourning. For the purpose of clarity, I'd suggest that mourning is the process that follows the diagnosis of grief. It's an intentional activity employed for the purpose of integrating a loss in a powerful and purposeful way. When we mourn well, it's possible to emerge on the other side with clarity and allow the loss to serve others and ourselves.

Through the years, I've worked with clients who have mourned the loss of loved ones. Many have relied on their religious heritage to engage in the disciplines of mourning. For centuries, these practices have promoted the ability to deal with loss. How these traditions are executed can vary, but they include the following themes:

- Slow down to a near stop!
- Tell the story.
  - The Truth and Reconciliation Commission of South Africa was successful largely because it allowed victims a chance to tell their stories. When we speak about what we feel, we regain agency and take control of our own world once again.
- Express emotions with freedom.
- Take additional time to reflect.
  - You might need to go fishing, play an extra round of golf, or spend some time in total quiet. Everyone reflects in her or his own way. Figure out what yours is.
- Care for your physical well-being.
  - The research on exercise leaves little doubt: Cardiovascular health correlates directly to emotional health. Get out and get moving.
- Receive the care of others.
- Take additional time to imagine.
- Slowly move forward.

AFTER GRIEVING AND MOURNING...RESILIENCE!

Ruth Davis Konigsberg is the author of the book *The Truth about Grief and the New Science of Loss*. The title would indicate that this isn't the type of book the typical leader would pull off the shelf for recreational reading on a Saturday afternoon. Konigsberg's work is significant because she challenges the longstanding view of grieving established by Elisabeth Kübler–Ross. She believes human beings are far more resilient than we give ourselves credit for and that most do not require assistance working through a grieving process. Her research reveals that a variety of factors shape an individual's ability to be resilient. Personality, beliefs, and socioeconomic factors greatly impact an individual's ability to recover from a loss and move forward with power and productivity.

If there are factors that assist leaders in being resilient, we should know what they are and embrace them in advance. We can be certain of one truth: In the course of our leadership lives, we will navigate loss multiple times. We will encounter that pain in a diversity of experiences. Therefore, why not prepare in advance?

There are a few things we can try to cultivate. Optimism has a profound effect on our ability to be resilient. Living with a sense of humility and awareness that we play an important role in a much bigger picture promotes resilience. Finally, having economic reserves can give us and our business the ability to take the time to mourn properly and be resilient. It's hard to take time to mourn when you have to worry about paying the rent and payroll. Building up a "rainy day" fund isn't just a good business idea; it's good preparation for personally rainy days of mourning.

I know how odd this chapter might seem in a "business book." It's unusual for any book to tell entrepreneurs to slow down, take time off, and step off the treadmill for just a bit. As entrepreneurs, we're far more comfortable in the world of strategy, sales, and success. The fact that we're comfortable, though, doesn't mean it's right. In fact, our ability to pursue these passions might be limited, thwarted, or lost because we didn't answer the wake-up call of loss. We all enjoy the economic benefit of producing value. You probably wouldn't be reading this book if you didn't. But also, we'll all deal with the pain of loss. Follow the guidelines in this chapter to help take those losses you encounter and make something better of them.

CHAPTER 6

YIKES!
THE WAKE-UP CALL
OF CHANGE

*Here's to the crazy ones. The misfits. The rebels.
The troublemakers. The round pegs in the square
holes. The ones who see things differently. They're
not fond of rules. And they have no respect for the
status quo. You can quote them, disagree with them,
glorify or vilify them. About the only thing you can't
do is ignore them. Because they change things.
They push the human race forward. And while some
may see them as the crazy ones, we see genius.
Because the people who are crazy enough to think
they can change the world, are the ones who do.*
—FROM APPLE'S "THINK DIFFERENT" CAMPAIGN

*Will you succeed? Yes, you will.
Ninety-eight and three-quarters guaranteed.*
—DR. SEUSS

STORY ONE: JEWELRY/EXCELLENCE/HUBRIS

In 1541, the Protestant religious reformer John Calvin banned the
wearing of jewelry. All of his followers, who collectively constituted
much of the region, observantly obeyed this ban, which unfortunately left the jewelers and goldsmiths of Switzerland out of work.

In response, those skilled tradesmen began making watches. This frantic shift to a changing market eventually led to greatness. After a few painstaking years of transition, Swiss watchmakers became the absolute best in the business.

For almost five hundred years, watches were made with tiny wheels. Those wheels rolled over each other mechanically, turning gears, all of which were powered by a spring that unwound slowly. The Swiss perfected this art; their watches were more reliable and accurate than any others. By 1968, Swiss watchmakers owned 65 percent of the worldwide market and 80 percent of the worldwide profits; they dominated the industry and were considered unstoppable. Swiss watches were status symbols; those who owned one clearly cared about quality. If you owned a different sort of watch, well, you didn't care much about watches. Within ten years, by 1978, the market share dominated by Swiss makers had shrunk to 10 percent. This precipitous decline in one industry adversely affected the entire national economy; 50,000 of the industry's 65,000 workers had to find other jobs. In that short span, the Japanese became the dominant force in watchmaking. Why did one region's dominance decline so sharply? How did this radical change happen? How did a people who had so aggressively seized upon an industry and adjusted to one change—Calvin—fail so completely to adjust to this new change?

In 1968, Swiss researchers presented a new technology to their companies that had been brewing in the timekeeper movement for years: the quartz movement. This new technology was totally electronic and at least ten times more accurate in telling time. It was also significantly cheaper. But the Swiss watchmakers rejected it. Their reactions were as follows: "Where are the gears? Where are the bearings? The mainspring? This isn't mechanically complicated, so how could it be the future of watches? It's a joke! Surely our customers appreciate our traditional methods and hard work. Who would be interested in this silly stuff? They buy our watches like an art collector buys art. They aren't looking for cheap knockoffs."

The Swiss were so confident that their way of making watches was unassailable that they didn't even patent the invention of quartz. Meanwhile, on the other side of the world, representatives from the Japanese company Seiko, *which had no share of the watch market in 1968,* saw this new technology at a trade show. They tinkered some with the design, put some of their best engineers on integrating it into a working product, and the rest is history. If you are wearing a watch today, chances are that it is powered through the technology that the Swiss disregarded as lacking art and sophistication. Chances are that you are thankful for the accurate timekeeping and for the fact that a watch is relatively affordable. Chances are that the Swiss, if they had a time machine, might regard that technology much differently now.

Story Two: A Family Inn, a Family Failure

Let's shift gears—forgive the pun—for a bit and go to another story. In this one, an immigrant—let's say he's an Irishman named Colin—comes to the United States. He sees in America a chance to control his destiny and create a brighter future for his family. Initially, Colin is broke after spending all of his savings on the journey. First and foremost, he needs to pay the rent and put food on the table. He settles in a community surrounded by fellow immigrants of Irish origin and takes a menial job in a factory. Through the years, Colin moves up slowly, but the opportunities for advancement are limited.

After years of working every weekday, and putting in some over-time, Colin's family reaches a level of stability. His wife does odd jobs and some cleaning on the wealthier side of town, and they somehow scrape together enough money to go on their first vacation as Americans. They decide to travel south along the old route US 1. The kids are thrilled!

After driving for most of the first day, the family decides to stop for the night. But they are unable to find a place to stay. As they drive around searching for a hotel, Colin suddenly has something of an epiphany. His family back in Ireland ran a small inn. Why couldn't he start a roadside lodge here in America? There are plenty of cars along these roads. Surely some of the other drivers want a place to break up their trip as well. Luckily—and this is probably the root of his idea—Colin knows what running an inn takes. He grew up watching his parents. He has stumbled on a market that needs something he can provide!

He scrapes together what savings he has managed to put together, drains the savings of his brothers and other family members with the promise to pay them back, and applies for a loan at the local bank. Colin's initial entrepreneurial endeavor includes only a few rooms, but he plans it well. He does his research and discovers the prime stopping places for north- and southbound travelers. He picks a site that is just less than a day's drive from two major cities. That way, people can travel a whole day from those two places and stop for a night. It is a fortuitous choice. His rooms are full every night, and he is able to charge higher and higher rates as the reputation of his hospitality and quality grows, along with the demand for rooms.

Within a few years, Colin has paid back his brothers and decides to expand. He builds ten more rooms and even a little breakfast diner. That way, he can attract travelers and locals as well. As cars get cheaper and travel becomes more accessible for larger swaths of the population, Colin's expanded business booms, regardless of how much he grows. Thirty years after his initial idea, Colin turns over his thriving business to his daughter (let's call her Abigail) and her husband. Abigail and her husband have essentially won a lottery—

they inherit a very stable business and the revenues that go along with it. They've inherited a life's work and their lives' calling. The combination of return guests and new faces provides a very high occupancy rate and a work environment that feels like working on the family farm. It is a lovely place.

In the early 1950s, Abigail starts to hear rumors about a new highway system that will allow people to travel both farther and faster. From a personal perspective, this second-generation immigrant family looks forward to the ability to travel to distant places. Abigail wants to visit Maine and hopes she might establish some sort of annual summer tradition where she takes the kids up to those rocky coasts where they can eat lobsters and do some sailing. She also thinks that faster travel might create more travelers. By the 1960s, a brand-new federal interstate connects New England to the Florida Panhandle, enabling drivers to go farther, faster. This interstate springs up only 3.5 miles from the family's thriving lodge and the old US 1. For those ten years, plenty of people eschew the interstate for a slower mode of travel. And, while she advertises near the interstate, Abigail finds her business just as successful as ever. But, by the 1970s, she begins to notice a subtle change in the business. Initially, the new faces stop in with less frequency. In time, the return visitors begin to disappear. They are staying instead at the chain hotels that seemed to spring up like unwelcome weeds every thirty miles along that new interstate, visible from the road itself.

By the early 1980s, it is more and more difficult to make ends meet. Abigail starts to encourage her children to make sure they look for a different future. After all, the family business is dying and is just around the corner from death. Having grown up in the hotel industry, those children go to work during their summers in the corporately owned hotel that was built near the exit of the interstate, just 3.5 miles from the family motor lodge. There, they are treated like cogs in a machine; their working knowledge of customer service and good practices is disregarded in favor of rote policies. Years later, the fourth generation of this family—Colin's great-grandchildren—ride past the dilapidated building at the four-way stop in town.

"What is that?" they might ask.

If they did, the answer would be, "That used to be our future."

From Watches and Hotels to You

The world of business is filled with stories of game-changing events that mark progress for one business and the end of another. Economist Joseph Shumpeter coined the phrase "creative destruction" to characterize the fundamental nature of capitalism. Shumpeter described it like this: "Capitalism, then, is by nature a form or method of economic change and not only never is but never can be stationary.... The fundamental impulse that sets and keeps the capitalist engine in motion comes from the new consumers, goods, the new methods of production or transportation, the new markets, the new forms of industrial organization that capitalist enterprise creates."

I don't know many people who would disagree with this argument after considering it for a minute or two. Capitalism is generally viewed as a dynamic and ever-shifting system. Any decent business-person understands this fact, knows that markets can be fluid, and realizes that consumers will track down quality and buy it! But in this capitalist country of ours, I've also heard just as many times as you have the common belief that *people do not change*. How can we rectify these two seemingly oppositional ideas? We live in a capitalist society, so things constantly change. Yesterday's America Online is today's Gmail. Today's Twitter is tomorrow's...who knows! Yet people are generally viewed as intransigent and unwilling to change. How is it that business empires have risen and fallen on both the power of change and resistance to change? More specifically, why were these Swiss watchmaking companies so irrationally sure that their share of the market was safe, especially after they'd so adeptly adjusted to the jewelry ban instituted by Calvin?

Chip and Dan Heath argue in their book *Switch* that people are not averse to change. Rather, life is marked by a series of changes that we embrace. We cheer for our children as they pull themselves off their crawling knees to walk. As teenagers, we all look forward eagerly to the freedoms of driving a car or heading off to college. Young adults in the workforce work long hours in search of their big break, their big promotion. The most hopeless of sports fans— Chicago Cubs fans, for instance—believe with every opening day that "this will be the year everything changes!"

Humans have a natural ability to embrace change, and even seek it, given the right set of circumstances. One might go so far as to suggest that seeking change is something of an instinct, particularly when we are young. This begs three questions: Why do so many entrepreneurs supervise dying businesses because of their failure to adapt to shifts in their particular markets? Why do so many organizations fail to implement change successfully? If change is natural, why is it so difficult?

A simple change such as a new highway can have seismic consequences on an old business. Our blindness or resistance to change can render us irrelevant. Therefore, we must heed the wake-up call of change. We must use this inevitable fact of the universe to our advantage and not our detriment. Below are belief statements you may want to adopt to help you answer the constant call of change. They can help you avoid hitting the snooze button.

Can People Change?

In the face of the stories above, it might be fair to ask, "Can people change? Or are we forever swimming upstream, uncomfortable in new surroundings?" The short answer is: Of course people can change. The longer answer, and the one rooted in science, is this: It's complicated. When thinking about changing, it's helpful to think about the routines and habits everyone develops. Most researchers say it can take three to four weeks to break a habit. That's the amount of time it takes to make the basal ganglia—the part of the brain that controls habitual behavior—to start firing differently. To make things more complicated, those old networks of neurons don't go away. So, once you've quit smoking or splurging on those potato chips, you have to go back only once to get the habit fired up again. In an online article, author Charles Bryant says, "You may reverse the way your neurons fire when you cease to smoke, but they'll change back immediately once you take that first puff. A 2009 study from the UK Health Behavior Research Centre indicated that it takes sixty-six days to genuinely make or break a habit, to the point where that new habit becomes your default behavior." *

If we think of embracing change as breaking an old behavior pattern and setting a new "default behavior," it can indeed take a while. In the case of the Swiss watchmakers, it might have taken ten or twelve more meetings with their brilliant engineers. It might have taken hours more of those engineers who'd discovered the uses for quartz banging the drum over and over, saying, "This can be useful! You should look into this!" In the case of Abigail and her husband, it might have taken time for them to acquaint themselves with the inevitability that faced them about the family inn. It might have taken numerous hard conversations with their children, who could

---

* Charles W. Bryant, "Are People Capable of Change?" How Stuff Works website, http://people.howstuffworks.com/are-people-capable-of-change1.htm.

perhaps see the new horizon a bit more clearly than their emotionally fraught parents. Sometimes you just have to keep plugging away.

In my work as a consultant, I've grown very familiar with the fact that some people are better at dealing with change than others. It seems like there are personality types out there that are either change-averse or change-friendly. To use the language of Meyers–Briggs's fourth preference pair, some people prefer a more "structured and decided lifestyle," while others want a more "flexible and adaptable" approach. Certainly some people need more structure in their lives than others, so they might feel a bit more anxious about constant evolutions in a business. But even people who value stability can deal with change. They just need that change charted better for them. All they want is to know, when going through a change process, what they can rely on, what they can lean on.

The most exciting thing I've discovered in my years of working on these topics, and doing research for that work, is that the oldest among us can change as well. We tend to think that young kids are more capable of learning than those who are older. Kids learn so much in those first few years that any subsequent growth and progression pales in comparison; that much is true. But we don't just get stagnant after our thirties. I didn't always feel this particular way. I'd often thought that people were pretty much who they were once they'd graduated from college. The accompanying implication was that older employees could be a bit more locked into the status quo, harder to motivate on new initiatives and train for new techniques. But plenty of research suggests that the brain remains plastic throughout one's life and can continue to change—physically and developmentally—even later in adulthood.

Let's take a scientific detour for just a second. The part of the brain that does the thinking and processing is known casually as "gray matter." The part that transmits messages is called "white matter." One recent scientific study found that even in older graduate students, the brain's makeup was changing in fundamental ways as they "learned." The "white matter" components of the brain increased a great deal during the course of new learning opportunities. That happened because the students were forging new communication networks between the white and gray parts of their brain. Those new connections are…learning! To reiterate, consider this comment about a Dartmouth University study: "Now that we actually do have tools to watch a brain change, we are discovering that in many cases the brain can be just as malleable as an adult as it is when you are a child or an adolescent."*

Anecdotally, I'd argue that the most essential elements for a changed perspective are curiosity and the ability to self-reflect. Some people seem to be more curious—whether that perspective is innate or learned—than others. Those who are both curious and able to understand how their actions will appear to others are more flexible than others. But everyone has triggers that a good leader can activate. Everyone can change. The next sections of this chapter deal with some of the consistent responses to change and some of the stages you'll have to move people through. I'll end with a focus on some of the constants you can give to others to alleviate their discomfort as you push for major new initiatives in a changing world.

Standard Responses to Change

Coping with change isn't as easy as is sometimes suggested. We may read Colin and Abigail's story about the family inn and think of all the ways they should've responded proactively. "They should've adjusted to a changing market," we might mutter. It's one thing to

---

* Janice Wood, "You Can Teach an Old Dog New Tricks," PsychCentral website, last modified September 27, 2012, http://psychcentral.com/news/2012/09/27/you-can-teach-an-old-dog-new-tricks/45219.html.

read the broad strokes of their narrative and judge. But it's quite another thing for Abigail to uproot her family and move closer to the interstate. She would've certainly absorbed some short-term financial losses to make profits in the long term. Those longer-term profits were by no means guaranteed. The difficulties were not all financial, either. She would've been abandoning the building that her father built and thus would've walked away from her family's history, in some ways. Those sorts of things are not easy. In the case of the watchmakers, many of those individuals had spent a lifetime perfecting a craft that was—with this recommendation for changed techniques—being implicitly rendered obsolete. When faced with these emotionally difficult components of change, it can be hard to pull the proverbial trigger. Abigail and her husband exemplify many of Dr. A. J. Schuler's reasons that people tend to be risk-averse about change. Let's look at those ten reasons through the lens of the family inn story:

1. **The risk of change is seen as greater than the risk of standing still**—What if Abigail packs up and moves the business and they lose all their old customers?

2. **People feel connected to other people who are identified with the old way**—Abigail's family established this business. Abigail remembers waking up on Christmas morning there as a child. It isn't easy to leave that kind of comfort.

3. **People have no role models for the new activity**—What sorts of different business practices will be necessary to attract the faster-moving clientele of the interstate? This sort of hotel environment isn't what Abigail knows

and does well, and she isn't altogether that interested in changing her methods.

4. **People fear that they lack the competence to change—** Can Abigail and her husband pull it off?

5. **People feel overloaded and overwhelmed—**Rarely have I met someone who felt underworked or not busy enough. We can get so wrapped up in the day-to-day operations of the status quo that we fail to account for the changes we need to enact. Abigail and her husband surely worried more about what buildings needed painting or what rooms needed renovation than they did about the metachanges they should've been considering. In the face of busy tasks, it can be hard to step away and look at the forest rather than just zone in on the trees.

6. **People have a healthy skepticism and want to make sure that new ideas are sound—**Abigail remembers when a new bed and breakfast sprang up down the road. Her parents felt tremendous pressure to lower their prices. But they stuck with their model of quality service and high-end lodging. It was tight for a while, but eventually that competitor shut down. Will this interstate be a fad? Will people move back to slower travel soon enough?

7. **People have hidden agendas among would-be reformers—**Maybe Abigail starts to notice a split among her children; one wants her to move and the other wants her to stay. She can be pressured each way and can hardly view the situation objectively.

8. **People feel that the proposed change threatens their notion of themselves**—This hotel is her family. She doesn't know what she would do without it.

9. **People anticipate a loss of status or quality of life**—Sure, business is slowing down. But a move involves a risk that business will dry up and fail altogether. It can be easier to choose death by a thousand pricks than to gamble with more aggression.

10. **People genuinely believe the proposed change is a bad idea.***—Maybe Abigail's husband firmly believes that moving toward the interstate will never work, that a new sort of advertising policy might help them recover some of their lost business, etc.

I listed and explained these ten common reasons to resist change through the example of our hotel story, but some of them apply in almost every failure to adopt change. Many of the reasons in this list of ten involve people's emotions and memories. Always remember that you as an entrepreneur are susceptible to them, too! When you are confronting a major change initiative, or thinking about taking a major new direction in your business, you'll do well to think of these emotional responses. Schuler argues that this emotional component of change is the one that "would-be change agents" understand most poorly. But when leaders are trying to move themselves toward a new change, or are trying to motivate others, they need to appeal to rational thought as well.

Let's look at another model as one step toward integrating the rational and emotional dimensions of change—one that involves

---

* http://www.schulersolutions.com/index.html.

walking employees through various levels of resistance toward new initiatives.

STANDARD RESPONSES IN THE WORKPLACE

The types of responses listed above apply to work, but they might also apply to many elements of life outside the office setting. To look a bit more specifically at that, and to give you another lens, Robert Bacal, an author, speaker, and consultant, has identified four different "stages" that people undergo in the workforce as they are confronted by change. Bacal's stages pertain a bit more specifically to what a leader will face when trying to lead and implement change. These stages bear some resemblance to Elizabeth Kübler–Ross's stages of grief, discussed in Chapter 5, on the wake-up call of loss. Bacal's stages are as follows and are characterized by people's common reactions to change:

1. Denial:
   • "We've seen stuff like this before."
   • "This is another half-baked idea from leadership."
   • "This phenomenon will pass."

2. Anger and resistance:
   • "Who does she think she is, making me do this?"
   • "What was wrong with the way things were?"
   • "I'm not going to do x." "Why pick on us?"

3. Exploration and acceptance
   • "Well, I guess we should make the best out of it."
   • "Let's get back to work."
   • "I'll have to make it work."

4. Commitment:

- People really start to move forward with the change, get fully on board, and are eager to help…until the next big change!*

It is important for leaders to recognize that these stages are, in many ways, inevitable. People will almost always experience some of them when confronted with major shifts in their lives at work. Do you have the tools to help employees, and yourself, move through these stages productively?

BREAKING OTHERS OUT OF THE CYCLE

I read an article in *Harvard Business Review* about the various ways you can help others embrace change. It summarized nicely some of the various approaches I've used in the past. The article argued that you should simplify goals. When you have twenty goals, you actually have none. So you should "embrace the power of one." Once you've established a limited number of goals, you should attempt to make sure those goals are "sticky." Goals for change shouldn't be vague. They should have particular and traceable components. The article talked, as well, about the importance of framing this change within a vivid story or picture. Part of what makes great leaders great is their capacity to draw others into their narrative. Can you frame change as an opportunity to be leveraged rather than as a thing to be feared, and can you do so within the story employees already situate themselves within?

From a traditional HR sense, you can always use the age-old "carrots" and "sticks" to motivate people. You have surely read Daniel Pink and probably agree with his finding that intrinsic (internal) motivation is much more effective for creative behaviors than

---

* Robert Bacal, "Understanding the Cycle of Change, and How People React to It," Work911 website, http://work911.com/articles/changecycle.htm.

extrinsic (external) motivation. But using pay, bonuses, and promotions (extrinsic rewards) can help get people on board for certain tasks. I am also of the opinion that, at times, you have to recognize those people who aren't on board with the changes you want and that you make personnel changes when necessary. (Translation: Know when to fire people who just don't get it!)

Some of the article's recommendations bear a lot of resemblance to the arguments of Malcolm Gladwell's *Tipping Point*. You can "activate peer pressure" and mobilize larger crowds if you find the right people to help you start a movement. Many change initiatives work better if they feel organic and bottom-up rather than top-down mandates. Figure out ways to mobilize the rank-and-file employees; give them ownership of the changes by involving them early in the process. Gladwell's *Tipping Point* is essentially about that moment when a change evolves from something small and personal to something much bigger. Gladwell talks a great deal about "mavens" and "salesmen" who facilitate and enable change to grow. Mavens are sort of "information specialists." They tend to accumulate knowledge, want to solve other people's problems, and act as information brokers. Salesmen, on the other hand, are persuasive, charismatic people who can convert other people. You will do well in your efforts to build change into your organization if you can recruit some of these two types of people to help you.

In addition to recruiting the right people, also consider tweaking the situation in a way that might shift behaviors. The HBR article tells of Google moving its salad bar to the front of the cafeteria line, based on the research that people tend to grab what they see first. They nudged their employees toward choices the employees wanted to make anyway.

If you're heeding the wake-up call, or a demand for change in your particular industry, you can use all of the techniques listed above to get others on board. Tell them a story that helps them see things like you see it. Recruit a team—what Harvard professor and change expert John Kotter would call a "coalition of the willing"—to help you get things off the ground. Tweak the situation to make success easier for people. Reward those who jump on board with you, and don't be afraid…. When people just won't wake up themselves, find new people!

USING HIGH-IMPACT PEOPLE AS CATALYSTS

I briefly discussed the notion of finding high-impact individuals to be a part of your initial coalition. This is a concept rich enough to merit further attention. Let's take a look at the "theory of diffusion." We've all known those people who always seem to have the newest gadget or who've heard about that hot new CD or book before anyone else. On the other side of the spectrum, we've all had friends who held on to their old cell phone until it's past its point of usefulness, who dodged a particular social phenomenon almost out of stubborn persistence. There's a theory that addresses the steps a person goes through when facing a new innovation. It's called "diffusion theory," and the five steps are as follows:

1. **Knowledge**—A person becomes aware of an innovation and has some idea of how it functions.

2. **Persuasion**—He or she forms a favorable or unfavorable attitude toward the innovation.

3. **Decision**—The person engages in activities that lead to a choice to adopt or reject the innovation.

4. **Implementation**—He or she puts an innovation to use.

5. **Confirmation**—The person evaluates the results of
a decision about an innovation he or she has already
made.*

The most striking feature of diffusion theory is that, for most
members of a social system, the innovation decision depends heavily
on the innovation decisions of the other members of the system.
After 10 to 25 percent of a system's members adopt an innovation,
the remaining members adopt the innovation relatively rapidly. Then
there is a period in which the holdouts finally adopt. In other words,
there are leaders within a system. Everyone else watches them and
looks for cues. Think about these questions as a way to frame change
more effectively: How do we usually hear about change? How do we
know it is coming?

True Change/Superficial Edits

In my work as a consultant, I've seen plenty of examples of what
I'd call "superficial edits" as opposed to "true change." I've seen
employees who have "complied" with change initiatives but are
still not fully invested. There are plenty of differences between
compliance, by the way, and cooperation. You want people to take
ownership of the business's success, to bring themselves fully to their
work. That doesn't happen if they are simply obeying edicts they
don't believe in.

Think about it this way: There's a big difference between the
following two questions:

1. Can you stop drinking so much?

---

* Everett Rogers, "Diffusion of Innovations," reviewed by Greg Orr, last modified
March 18, 2003, posted on the Stanford University website, http://www.stanford.
edu/class/symbsys205/Diffusion%20of%20Innovations.htm.

2. Can you fundamentally change your instinct to indulge
   in addictive behavior?

One of these questions—the first one—gets at superficial edits. Many people can stop drinking so much. They might be able to "comply" with that goal. But if they long for a drink every time they see someone else with a glass of wine, how effective have they been at changing their behavior?

The difference between real change and superficial change is extremely important in business. Salesmen are always better when they really believe in what they're selling. Employees will be more productive and have longer, more sustainable careers if they're doing something they believe is worthwhile. For those reasons, when I'm leading change initiatives, I'm not just looking for compliance. I'm looking for total buy-in. I'm looking for changes in employees that are real, not superficial.

CHANGING WORLD

My grandfather started his career as a bus driver at age twenty. He put in his thirty-five years as a driver for Greyhound, retired, and lived out his retirement on a nice little pension. He worked for his entire career at a single job and was happy for it! He never had to deal with wholesale industry change. But, just a generation later, things were starting to move a bit more quickly. My father graduated from college and went to work as an accountant. Early in his career, he learned how to do double-entry bookkeeping. But halfway through his career, Dad had to look his career future square in the eyes. He saw computers on the horizon, watched as they crept more and more into his job, and recognized pretty quickly that much of what he did would be automated in ten years. He had to adjust to the reality that his career trajectory would be different than his father's. He'd need to be much more adept at shifting and developing new skills. Those demands have only escalated today.

We live in a world today in which few industries are safe from major changes, from tectonic shifts in the way customers are reached and served, in the way work is done. Our goal, therefore, should be to work toward increased pliability. We want to be adept, to answer quickly the wake-up calls in our respective industries, to anticipate shifts just before they happen. We have to recognize that change is with us and make a bedrock commitment to approach everything in our lives with an insatiable sense of curiosity.

I know this much for sure: You're going to either live in the past or live in the future. You have to cultivate and develop a curiosity that causes you to learn. I've read of great businesses that initially establish goals geared toward diversifying funding streams and promoting innovation. Company X, for example, might aim to have 15 percent of its revenues come from new markets within ten years. How can you build innovation and a change-receptive stance into your business?

IN THE WINDS OF CHANGE, WHAT HOLDS FAST? UNCHANGING TRUTHS IN BUSINESS

I don't mean to paint a one-dimensional, or overly simplistic, picture of change as the only universal truth. Sure, most companies are dealing with technology or regulatory shifts and population trends. But universal and unchangeable truths of business exist as well. If you have mastered such truths, you could succeed in most any business. You just have to be able to think broadly enough and to apply those truths to your particular situation. If you can lock in on those, you'll feel safer. What are they?

Truth 1. Business is still about relationships

Facebook and Twitter have fundamentally altered the way most industries reach out to consumers, market their products, and communicate priorities. And, in some ways, social media has changed the way we think about "relationships." A "friend" on Facebook begs the question: What is the difference between that sort of relationship and the more traditional face-to-face relationship? Which types of connections are more meaningful? Sustainable?

One of the more publicized effects of social media has been in the organizational capacity built into systems. For example, the Arab Spring was a wave of revolutionary demonstrations and protests (both violent and nonviolent), plus riots and civil wars that began in the Arab world on December 18, 2010. The movement promoted incredible social change and was largely organized on Facebook and Twitter. Obviously, these tools have incredible power for business.

When you think about how to integrate "changes" into your model, also consider a broad problem with this new technology. Now that the government of Egypt has been overthrown through protests, discord and inefficiencies persist. The business of running that country will still flourish or fail along relational lines. Social media venues such as Facebook can never replace the power of human relationships. You might be able to orchestrate a gathering through Twitter or to communicate simplistic messages. But eventually, you need to go back to the business of interpersonal relationships.

As you navigate change, maintain trusting and productive relationships. Nurture them. If you do so well, you'll be better prepared for anything the winds of change might bring your way.

Truth 2. People will pay more for excellence

Target and Williams–Sonoma both sell kitchen implements. At each store, you can get coffeemakers, spatulas, kitchen towels, and more. If you needed some new pots and pans, you could get those at either place. But only at Williams–Sonoma can you buy a DeLonghi Prima Donna S. Super Automatic Espresso Maker. Such a purchase will put you out about $3,000, give or take tax. But you could make a killer espresso once you've laid out the cash! You could get knives for chopping vegetables at either store. But you probably aren't going to find a $500 knife at Target. What am I getting at here? I'm not picking on Williams–Sonoma or Target. But this example represents one of my eternal truths of business. People can get the same stuff at Target. But they can get *better* things at Williams–Sonoma. Both companies exist and are succeeding. Williams–Sonoma has survived a climate in which they are underbid by providing excellence.

Truth 3. People will always value customization

I recently saw some younger kids—in middle school, perhaps—wearing Nike high-top sneakers that had their names actually sewn into the tongues of the shoes. I visited Nike's website to find out how they'd done it. Nike now has an entire product line for people who want to "customize" their shoes. As you might imagine, customers pay a premium for that option. Nike has figured out a way to integrate its production capacity with customer choice. I'd hazard a guess that this sort of integration is the way of the future.

The department store Nordstrom—which also embodies Truth 2 as well—is a testament to this third truth as well. When you shop at Nordstrom, the sales clerks will actually *help* you select the right clothes for your body type. They will recommend things to you. They will customize your shopping experience through excellent customer service. Plenty of people in the world will pay for that sort of thing.

Target is worth a repeat appearance in this rule as well. Target isn't a higher-end company like Nordstrom or Williams–Sonoma. But it does sell designer products that are *quality* and affordable. When you buy something at Target, you can expect that it'll work like it should. And if it doesn't, you know you can return it for a decent customer-service experience. Target isn't going out of business anytime soon!

Conclusion

You'll have to face the wake-up call of change often as a leader. As you do, those three truths, if you can harness them, will serve you well, regardless of the industry you're in. Let's close with a couple of my beliefs.

1. I believe change is natural and necessary!

The forward movement of time and the inevitable change in seasons are both natural occurrences that illustrate the natural progress of history. Things move forward, and as they do, a natural evolution takes place. Caterpillars become butterflies, children become adults, and human ingenuity creates new technologies. Resistance is futile. Moreover, resistance obscures all of the beauty and possibility built into that change. Therefore, it is wise for us to embrace the reality of change and prepare ourselves to leverage it rather than fight against it.

2. I believe change is occurring now that will have a profound impact on my world!

You can trust that there's some revolutionary shift happening somewhere in the world that will eventually impact your business and your life. The most dangerous place to be is living in the land of denial and desire and coasting for too long. In today's world, every enterprise requires some allocation of time and money toward research and development. Read journals, go to conferences, speak

117

to experts, and always have an eye and an ear toward the disruptive event that will change your world.

3. The future can be better than the past

If change is indeed happening, and it is, it is also important to remember that such change might just usher in a better world! Let's make sure it does. The quote that started this chapter, from Apple's Steve Jobs, glorifies those who can envision a different sort of future—change leaders who are creative enough and diligent enough to call for something entirely new and different. When you couple that notion of change as a necessary and wonderful part of the world with Dr. Seuss's quote about believing in your own success—"Yes, you will!"—you can move mountains. I love that the good doctor does not put the odds at 100 percent. He says that the likelihood of success is "Ninety-eight and three-quarters guaranteed." Maybe he wrote it that way to fit his rhyme and meter. But I think he was also placing some demands on the reader. We have to work for success. It won't just come to us. What will you do to "work" toward embracing change? What will you do to heed your wake-up call of change in a positive and productive way?

CHAPTER 7

OH, YEAH!
THE WAKE-UP CALL
OF BELIEF

*"He does not believe that does not
live according to his belief."*
—Sigmund Freud

*"The more that you read, the more
things you will know.
The more that you learn, the more places you'll go."*
—Dr. Seuss

Aaron Sorkin's screenplay *A Few Good Men* is loaded with so many great lines that the film is still quoted more than twenty years after its initial release in 1992. One of the most famous lines from that movie was delivered by Col. Nathan R. Jessup, played by Jack Nicholson, when he was being examined by Lt. Daniel Kaffee, a lawyer played by Tom Cruise: "You can't handle the truth!" That line pops up all over the place in modern culture. When the movie was first released, my friends and I, when volunteering to do a particularly onerous or tedious task, would quote a portion of the film about military men who serve on the front lines in difficult times: "You want me on that wall. You need me on that wall!" Another scene from the film serves as a perfect line for our jumping-off point to discuss our final wake-up call in the life of an entrepreneurial leader. In the scene, Lt. Cdr. JoAnne Galloway, played by Demi Moore, is attempting to convince Lt. Kaffee that he should put Col. Jessup on the stand. She thinks it is essential for their case that Jessup confess that he ordered a "code red," the result of which was the accidental death of a soldier. Galloway challenges Kaffee during one of their late-night planning sessions with the question, "Do you believe he ordered the code red?" The seasoned attorney, Lt. Kaffee, responds a bit dismissively, "It does not matter what I believe; it only matters what I can prove!"

In his role as a prosecuting attorney, Cruise's character believes he must separate himself from his own personal biases and focus first and foremost on the elements of the case he can make others believe. It's perhaps a fair point from the perspective of a lawyer. It also presumes that Kaffee's beliefs are irrelevant in his efforts. I'd argue quite the opposite. I think that by embracing his belief, he might just make a better lawyer.

This line also begs an appropriate set of questions with which we can conclude this book. We started out with the Rorschach test, and I made the argument that how we interpret events—the various wake-up calls I've addressed in the book—can actually determine the impact of those events on our lives. So we are in some ways back to the beginning. Is this distinction between those things we feel in our gut and the ones we can demonstrate objectively to outsiders a valid one in the life of leaders? Does what you believe impact how you perform and lead? In other words, do beliefs matter? I'm confident that many people would answer affirmatively, "They certainly do!" You'd rightly argue that beliefs can motivate us to keep plugging forward in the face of difficulties; beliefs can catalyze energy and passion in working toward certain causes. Let's look at some examples of this in the scientific world.

The placebo effect is one irrefutable testament to the power of belief. You're probably anecdotally familiar with it. Essentially, the placebo effect is when individuals are given "fake" pills that they believe have therapeutic effects. But something weird happens when those patients take the so-called "sugar pills." The people given the fake pill often do better than people given no pill at all. In other words, if they think something works, that belief itself can start healing their body. One of the more common examples is with headaches. People who take a fake pill often report that their headache gets better faster. It doesn't stop with headaches. The placebo effect can change one's perception of pain as well as one's heartbeat, blood pressure, and digestion. If people believe they're getting better, they often do better in reality.*

I want to take this fact—that believing matters can impact your functionality in the world—as a given. And I want to talk about our final big wake-up call that correlates to this assumption. Are you optimizing the impact of your beliefs or learning to change your reality? Despite the ample research about how much belief impacts daily activities, many people find themselves, on a daily basis, functioning in a way that is totally incongruent with their core beliefs. Moreover, too many people fail to orchestrate their career path so that they can embody their core beliefs. Thus, they leave the power of belief underused.

Think of the doctors who practice medicine because they believe good health is important, but take smoke breaks throughout the

---

* "On the Brain: When Believing Is Healing," CNN website, last modified June 1, 2011, http://thechart.blogs.cnn.com/2011/06/01/on-the-brain-when-believing-is-healing/.

course of their day. A bit more nebulously, think of a doctor who could stand to lose a few pounds; he strolls into an exam room and tries to convince a patient of the increased risk for heart disease that obesity causes. I'm reminded of that old line parents said to their children when hypocrisy became evident: "Don't do as I do; do as I *say* do!" One of my first clients was an estate planner who had no will in place for his family. How could he base his entire life on the necessity of good planning and fail to do it himself? This level of hypocrisy is not a new phenomenon. The old phrase, "The cobbler's kid has no shoes" reveals that such inconsistencies between one's life work and one's daily actions is nothing new.

There's no doubt that life has a way of creating a misalignment between our beliefs and our most common practices. We cherish our families, but are kinder to strangers. We understand growth is important, but prefer our ruts and resist change. Therefore, it's possible that one of the wake-up calls we so desperately require is the alarm of hypocrisy. Our final wake-up call is that "Oh, yeah!" moment.

First, we will discuss the nature of beliefs and how they impact our world view and daily activities. Then, we will examine that moment—we've all faced it to some extent—when we realize that we're living and functioning in a way that's incongruent with our beliefs. Finally, I want to take things a step further. When you're acting according to your beliefs, and it's not working, how open are you to changing your perception? How open are you to a conversion?

BELIEFS AS A LENS

A story is told in many churches once every few years of a religious man who finds himself on top of a roof during a great flood. He's a man of great devotion, and even as he's driven by the rising waters from the bottom floor of the house out the window and up to the roof, he doesn't fear. Luckily, a man comes by in a boat and says, "Get in, get in. I'll take you to safety!" But, to this generous man's surprise, the stranded man on top of his roof in a rising tide replies, "No need. I have faith in God; he will grant me a miracle."

The man in the boat motors away. A few hours go by, and this man of faith waits patiently as the water starts to creep up the roofline. A few hours later, the man is up to the apex of his roof. Thankfully, another boat comes by. The pilot of that boat tells him, "Climb aboard!" The man responds, once again, that he has faith in God, and God will grant him a miracle. Once the water has reached his ankles, this man starts to hear the whirl and hum of a helicopter's rotors. He soon sees the chopper and watches as it makes its way toward him. With the water now reaching his knees, someone in the helicopter throws down a ladder and announces over the loudspeaker that he should just climb up. Once again, the man turns down the request for help because of his faith of God.

So this religiously devout man does what we expect: He drowns. When he arrives at the gates of heaven, his faith is shattered. He has been proven wrong and died for his mistake. In his mind, God has let him down, has not rewarded him for his faith. He was not saved. As he stands before those pearly gates, he says to Peter, "I thought God would grant me a miracle, and I have been let down." St. Peter chuckles somewhat sympathetically and responds, "I don't know what you're complaining about. We sent you two boats and a helicopter."

This story derives some of its popularity from the fact that it represents some truisms. We often can't separate ourselves from our own perception of things; we can't see reality without our own particular lens. This man could not see miracles for what they were. He wanted something more grandiose than a plain boat. He couldn't see just how salvific that boat was for him at that moment.

Research supports this modern little parable. What we believe *does* matter. Studies reveal that our beliefs heavily shape what we are able to hear and how we interpret the events around us. They become major factors in how we eventually make decisions. James Rieley has studied the impact of beliefs in the workplace. Some of his research is covered in the book *Gaming the System*. In that work, Rieley argues, "We don't believe the world we see; we see the world we believe." Rieley argues that the way we formulate our beliefs is a slow and steady process. What we "know" becomes validated as "truth" when we subtly but surely look for data that support our beliefs and dodge the data points that undermine our assumptions. The fancy word for this is "confirmation bias," but it is also casually referred to as "myside bias." Over time, this phenomenon becomes a reinforcing dynamic.

In this cycle, the stronger our beliefs, the more we look for supporting evidence that our beliefs are the right ones. This activity makes those beliefs stronger, causing us to look for more proof, and so on. This plays out in the world in myriad ways. An easy and simple way to think of it, though, is that the Fox News audience rarely turns the channel to MSNBC. You'd find yourself hard-pressed, on the other hand, to find an MSNBC viewer watching Britt Hume without a grimace on his or her face. Those two "news" channels become a sort of echo chamber in which facts begin to be increasingly overshadowed by beliefs.

Rieley isn't the first to argue this sort of thing. A classic 1970s study by some Stanford scientists titled "Biased Assimilation and Attitude Polarization: The Effects of Prior Theories on Subsequently Considered Evidence" showed similar findings. In this study, people who were avowed pro- or anti-death penalty were exposed to two fake scientific studies. One of those fake studies intrinsi-cally supported the death penalty by suggesting that rates of crime were lower in cultures that had capital punishment. The other fake study undermined the notion that capital punishment deters violent crime and, in particular, murder. Both groups—the pro- and anti-death penalty folks—were asked to comment on the studies, which had been written to be equally strong. Each group tended to criticize the study whose conclusions disagreed with their own much more heavily, while describing the study that was more ideologically congruent as more "convincing."*

If we have a predisposition regarding the integrity of a leader, it will influence how we interpret the words of that leader. Every time the president of the United States speaks, those who supported his election are assured and comforted by his words. Simultaneously, those same words reinforce the reasons why others do not support him. It doesn't matter much what he says for the listener. This sort of bias—which so many of us suffer from—makes it very difficult for any of us to become converts. We're not easily convinced by "facts" because we see every fact through our own particular lens.

Our brains are far from perfect computers. They have a unique capacity to become emotionally entangled with ideas we believe to be true. They're unable to refrain from shading "facts" with preconceptions. Furthermore, we can emotionally reject any ideas we believe to be false and be done with them, even if they merit further consideration. This dynamic forms two distinct types of bias that will shape every aspect of our learning: behavior and performance. The first I discussed above. The flip side of that first bias merits some attention as well.

---

* Charles G. Lord, Lee Ross, and Mark R. Lepper, "Biased Assimilation and Attitude Polarization: The Effects of Prior Theories on Subsequently Considered Evidence," *Journal of Personality and Social Psychology*, 1979, 2098-2109, posted on the Princeton University website, http://synapse.princeton.edu/~sam/lord_ross_lepper79_JPSP_biased-assimilation-and-attitude-polarization.pdf.

1. **Confirmation bias**—The first type of bias is discussed briefly above. This bias causes us to pay more attention and assign greater credence to ideas that support our current beliefs. In other words, we cherry-pick the evidence that supports a contention we already believe and ignore evidence that argues against it.

2. **Disconfirmation bias**—The opposite side of that problem is just as vexing. In disconfirmation bias, we expend disproportionate energy trying to disprove ideas that contradict our current beliefs.

SOMETIMES BELIEFS DON'T WORK FOR US

At a recent family gathering, I watched as two of my relatives—one a conservative and one a liberal—debated all sorts of issues. They moved from topic to topic, pontificating on each in much the way you might expect if you ever watch political debates on television. I was drawn away from the conversation at some point, to go help with the dishes. When I came back, I asked one of them, "Did you win? Did he finally give in and admit that you were right?" The response was what you would probably expect: Neither party had "given in." Neither had convinced the other. They'd simply gone through the motions and walked away much the same as they'd entered the conversation. Neither person had seen the logic of the other, and neither rethought some tenets of his own philosophy.

I believe, in both politics and business, we too rarely open ourselves up to significant shifts in thinking. One fact of the world is…we are often wrong! But in those moments when we're confronted with logic from another perspective, we don't usually relinquish our deepest biases and change our conceptions of the world. My question to my relative was meant to be funny, but it was rooted in a deep frustration. I don't know that I've ever watched one of those debates on cable television between liberal and conservative pundits and heard the phrase, "You know, you are right. I need to rethink things." The reality is, one side usually ought to revisit his or her argument. It would be so refreshing in a debate between presidential candidates to hear, "On that matter in the past, I was wrong. I've had to rethink my position in the light of new data and facts. I've changed my mind thoughtfully."

This resistance to revisiting our beliefs is a particularly virulent problem in the world of entrepreneurship and business. We must be constantly open to alternate views; no philosophy or strategy should be sacrosanct in this ever-changing world! With that in mind, let's move to a rather provocative section on conversion.

ARE YOU A CONVERT?

My challenge to you, dear reader, is to ask yourself just how thoroughly your biases have engrained themselves in your overarching perception of the world. Although biases in our brains are natural and make us human, they can be problematic if they prevent us from being awake. So, just when was the last time you were converted?

If the evidence is clear, our beliefs shape what we learn and what we hear. If our beliefs impact the way we digest the world around us, and eventually the decisions we make, it begs the following questions: Do your beliefs serve you well? Could your current level of performance be a reflection of ineffective beliefs you've drifted toward by living in a world thoroughly committed to your mediocrity? Is it possible that your daily conduct doesn't really reflect what you actually believe? If that's the case, what would it be like to work for someone like you? What must your employees think of that obvious hypocrisy? If you're acting according to your beliefs and failing, should you revisit those beliefs?

In each of the previous chapters, I've suggested that the natural course of events in life have a way of either debilitating your leadership or catapulting it into new and better terrains. These events can sound an alarm that awakens the leader in each of us. Might I suggest that the alarm is ringing, too, if it has been a long time since your last conversion? Far too many leaders have lost their effectiveness because their biases are preventing a new way of seeing, hearing, and deciding. When was the last time you were truly converted?

You May Need a Conversion If...

Jeff Foxworthy's humorous "You might be a redneck if..." performances took the country by storm in the mid-1990s. Maybe we could use that same concept to think about the need for conversion. When I use the word "conversion," I'm using the term to suggest a course correction. It's far more than a change of belief. The hallmarks of conversion involve creating a new set of emotional entanglements around a truth. New patterns of habits are formed; new investments of time are made; and greater linkage among the head, the heart, and personal conduct is established. So if any of the following might be true, I'd suggest the alarm is sounding, and it might be time for your conversion:

1. Your actions are incongruent with your stated beliefs.

2. You're rejecting the contributions of a person who's respected by people you respect.

3. You're struggling with clarity, meaning, and purpose.

4. There's a high level of conflict in your most important relationships.

5. You've flatlined in your personal growth and
   development.

This list is far from exhaustive, but it's a good starting point for
you to consider.

Conversion—How?

Converting isn't as easy as deciding to know something new. As
with anything in life worth having, it takes some work to get there.
The following list gives you some options for seeking productive
conversions.

1. **Identify your core beliefs and write them in a statement**—One thing any good leader ought to do every few
   years is develop a statement of personal mission. What
   is it that you would do if you could be your own vision
   of a perfect leader every day? Before you can answer
   that question, you have to have some conception of what
   a good leader is. So try to construct a list of what you
   really believe. Start with a top-ten list—an individually
   designed "ten personal commandments of leadership."
   You might believe in delegating assignments to talented
   people to develop your bench. You might believe in
   approaching change as an opportunity rather than a
   challenge. You might list as one of your commandments the importance of listening twice as much as
   talking. This list will vary depending on your industry
   and personality. You might believe in paying your high
   performers well and generating a certain degree of churn
   with low performers. Once you've drafted your list, you
   might ask yourself, "Am I abiding by these command-

ments? Do my daily routines fit within my conception of what a good leader does?"

2. **Find a teacher, coach, or mentor**—Sometimes the easiest way to search for a conversion is to listen to those people we trust. If you don't already have a teacher, coach, or mentor, seek one out. Be methodical about talking with them. Set up a regular coffee or golf game that gives them the opportunity to "convert" you to something new! Once you've found them, be proactive about seeking from them constructive feedback rather than one-dimensional compliments.

3. **Involve yourself in a community of high-performing leaders**—If you've been to business school or have spoken with a recent graduate, they'll often tell you that the most valuable portion of their experience wasn't the classes or lectures. Often, it wasn't even the readings, as valuable as they are. Usually, the most valuable part of a good graduate-school experience is surrounding one's self with a diverse array of smart and motivated people. When you're surrounded by people who are motivated to do well and have the capacity to do so, your own performance will increase. And you'll have plenty of opportunities to "convert" one of your particular routines or philosophies to those you hear from others.

4. **Read outside your typical genres**—Some of the myth around the experience of conversion is that it's not something you find. The mistaken assumption is that conversion has to find you, à la Paul on his road to Damascus. Can we cognitively diagnose the fact that we

are in need and thus go out shopping for a new set of beliefs and practices? Regarding most of the knowledge out there that could be useful to us, we don't even know that we don't know it.* One way to get outside our own lens and explore new things is to read books in a genre we might otherwise ignore, to try to cultivate unique hobbies that seem totally disconnected from our routines. The ancient Samurai, who were some of the greatest warriors and swordsmen the world has ever known, focused a great deal on the martial arts and on honing their fighting skills. Surely in doing so, they improved their conditioning and fitness. But they also took classes in calligraphy, bonsai cultivation, tea ceremonies, origami, flower arranging, and painting. Think of that for a second—fierce warriors doing origami! Those warriors knew that all sorts of wisdom could be found outside of their particular genre of work. You can do something similar by picking up a book you might not otherwise read. What can you learn from it? What can you apply to your context as a seeker of conversion?

5. **Solicit feedback from other leaders**—This is pretty straightforward; one thing that can prompt a continual attitude of conversion is seeking feedback from those you respect. You have to come into these conversations eager to learn and humble about what advice others give you. Hubris is counterproductive when seeking feedback. And often, you have to invite constructive feedback actively to overcome people's natural inclination to avoid confrontation. Ask other leaders, "What should I/we be doing

---

* "Knowing Knowledge," Science in a Can website, http://sciencesoup.tumblr.com/post/41478027076/knowing-knowledge-my-math-teacher-always-used-to.

differently? What are we not considering?" Are there hidden efficiencies you might seek to exploit?

6. **Hang out in new places**—One thing I've noticed that's common in Western society is that traveling the world over is the purview of students. For many individuals, that's the time to study abroad, to indulge in wander-lust, to go out and see the world. This trend works well for people at that age. They don't have as many work and family responsibilities, and they have the maturity (for the most part) to go out on their own. It also works because we view college as a time of learning and explo-ration. Seeing new sights, hearing new sounds, smelling the cooking of a meal in India or Morocco can awaken creative inclinations and teach in a way that a classroom can't. After college, most travel takes place in retire-ment. I understand that family and work responsibilities can tether us to a place, that people in the midst of their careers have less flexibility. But I think that one of the best ways to seek conversion is to explore new places. Make it a priority to visit a place that is completely new to you. This place doesn't have to be all the way around the world. It could be an antique shop on the other side of town or a new ethnic restaurant. Regardless, make exploration of new places part of your routine. It will open you up to all sorts of conversion opportunities!

7. **Allocate time to read, study, and learn**—This is pretty much an amalgamation of all the other steps above, but a good leader has to make time in a day short on hours to open herself up to conversion. We have to create time in our schedules—literally block it off in your calendar!—

to learn and read and study. The greatest mistake working people make is failing to give themselves time to continue in their professional growth. It takes hours to learn new things! It takes stepping outside of the humdrum of our routines and investing in the opportunity to learn something new! Only then can you begin to have ideas about my last suggestion.

8. **Experiment with new ways of dealing with situations—** It's probably unnecessary to explain what this might look like. This suggestion is actually kind of a conclusion to the previous seven. You have to explore new opportunities for conversion, put yourself in new scenarios, and learn new things before you know what you'd like to experiment with. But once you've found something you think might work for you, it's time to try it out! I've been a proponent of "stretch" plans for leaders, where they develop strategies or styles they'd like to "try out" for a while. Once you've been converted to the possibility of something new, experiment it in your own daily life as a leader.

In a more concise form, here's that list again:

1. Identify your core beliefs and write them in a statement.

2. Find a teacher, coach, or mentor.

3. Involve yourself in a community of high-performing leaders.

4. Read outside your typical genres.

5. Solicit feedback from other leaders.

6. Hang out in new places.

7. Allocate time to read, study, and learn.

8. Experiment with new ways of dealing with situations.

CONVERSION AS A PROCESS

Usually, conversion is viewed as more of an event than a process. But I would argue that conversion is the unique interplay of right circumstances, right timing, and human will. By trying out the eight hints above, you can put yourself in a position for success. You can open the doors to the possibility of conversion. We must put ourselves in positions to encounter the truth that'll transform our effectiveness as leaders. If that alarm is ringing in your soul, and you need a conversion, try one of those techniques above. Step outside of your own lens of the world, or the way you think leadership should work, and try something new. Be like the Samurai warrior who finds his way to glory on the battlefield through arranging flowers. Pursue conversion!

CONCLUSION

We've talked in this chapter about how the "Oh, yeah!" wake-up call can take place when you recognize that your beliefs aren't necessarily reflected in your actions. That idea—that at times we stumble through life doing things we wouldn't do if we stepped outside ourselves for a moment—applies as well to all of the wake-up calls discussed in this book. In fact, the way I've talked about conversion in this chapter can help us tie all of our wake-up calls together.

Conversion, as discussed above and as it's viewed in the modern religious context, is the process of learning something new and channeling it in your own life. But it's also a methodology for taking those previous wake-up calls and channeling them into growth. Things happen to you. As discussed in the introduction, &%#@ happens. How can you convert the wake-up calls into growth and avoid stagnation? I look at the seven wake-up calls in this book as inevitable. We will *all* experience some of them in our lives. What do you need to be doing to prepare for them? I want to address, as the conclusion to this book, how we can take a conversion perspective when we face wake-up calls in our own lives.

CONVERSION AND THE OTHER WAKE-UP CALLS

Ah-Ha! (Insight)—What does conversion look like as it relates to insight? A counterproductive way of interpreting insight is that, in this flash of insight, we have a complete package. A conversion perspective means reinterpreting that insight as the beginning. That flash of understanding or new idea is the start. But it certainly isn't a sign of completion. We must convert the power of that insight to get to other insights, to make the original ideas work. Insight isn't an end. It's a means to the beginning of a journey.

Eureka! (Success)—I talked in the Eureka! chapter about the wake-up call of success and how it often can lead to some degree of apathy—the notion that one has made it and thus can stop trying. My argument, and the conversion perspective of success, is that success actually allows you to pursue a new set of success measurements. One should strive to look further, to redefine his or her purpose. The get-out-of-debt guru Dave Ramsey has incorporated something of the conversion perspective into his system. First, he argues, people should get out of debt. Once they've achieved a level of comfort and are debt-free, then they start giving to charities. At each benchmark, Ramsey's disciples are charged with redefining success in their current financial climate. In a start-up business, you are just a consumer of money. You have pretty much all expenses and very little revenue. Once you finally start to make it, you need to redefine what your goals are quickly. Convert your goals to something bigger and better to reach more and more success.

Cha-ching! (Money)—Money is not the root of all evil, but love of money is. Many false interpretations regarding the value, use and importance of money have shipwrecked lives. The entire journey of life requires a series of conversions related to how we allow money to impact us, and how we allow money to impact the world.

Uh-oh! (Failure)—Everything within us might naturally interpret a failure as a final outcome. What good could possibly come from landing flat on your face? A willingness to allow your beliefs regarding a failure to be converted could allow you to see the momentary event in the context of a much larger picture. Can you struggle to view failure as a part of a long-term development strategy?

Oh, no! (Loss)—Death is one arena where, historically, faith and belief have been naturally applied to address the pain of loss. However, faith and belief are powerful tools to reinterpret the variety of losses we encounter throughout the course of life. Are there some losses that are worthy of conversion?

Yikes! (Change)—If the brain has a way of interpreting all change as loss, then it's understandable how we fight change. Change is extremely fertile soil for conversion to take place, yet everything within us desires to cling to ineffective beliefs during a season of change. It's possible, if not necessary, to seek and experience conversion within our already existing beliefs while everything around us is changing. Can you change in the midst of change? Yes! Sometimes, you must!

Do It Yourself!

I could go through each of the seven wake-up calls of this book and explain what a conversion mentality might look like in that particular context. In fact, when I started writing this final chapter, I started to do just that. But I think applied knowledge and a working understanding are always better than unapplied knowledge.

My final challenge to you, the reader, is to think about what a conversion approach to those wake-up calls might look like. What way of interpreting failure is possible if we choose the path of conversion? What is the typical response to change, and how might you view it as an opportunity to convert old ways into better ones? What opportunities and obligations for transformation does money entail? What losses have you faced in your own life that you have confronted unproductively? What might a more productive—conversion—approach look like?

You will face wake-up calls in your business life. They are functionally neutral events, although some of them might entail sadness, grief, joy, or excitement. But once those events have happened, you have an obligation to your employees, to yourself, and to your family to convert them into further growth. If you do that, it'll show up in your bottom line. It'll show up in your productivity. It'll show up in your capacity to inspire others. It'll show up! Wake up the right way. Continue to grow. Be the best entrepreneur and leader you can be!

✍ ABOUT THE AUTHOR ✍

GLENN GUTEK IS the founder of Awake Consulting & Coaching, an organization devoted to helping professionals wake up and lead in the direction of excellence. The vision and passion he brings to Awake has shaped a team that brings unparalleled professionalism and expertise to making a bottom-line impact in the businesses and practices served by that team. With a variety of resources, Awake Consulting & Coaching has the ability to create a profitable business that serves clients, customers, staff, employees, and owners with enjoyment and excellence.

Before starting Awake Consulting & Coaching, Glenn worked with Atticus Practice Management Systems, a leading training and development firm devoted to the legal profession. He continues to function as a Senior Practice Advisor with Atticus, coaching attorneys to market their firms, reduce time consumed by the practice, and minimize stress in the practice. The experience of working with attorneys and his background in organizational development give Glenn a unique combination of education and experience that produces results for entrepreneurs, executives, and professionals. His skills in leadership, speaking, and training have placed him in the position to work with a wide array of leaders and entrepreneurs across the country.

Not only has Glenn studied the concepts and principles of great leadership and effective organizations, he has been a practitioner as well. For ten years, he served as a senior pastor with churches in

Southern California and Florida. In that setting, the skills and character attributes necessary to develop disciplined talent, align limited resources, communicate a clear vision, and mobilize a volunteer army were discovered and employed. The varied background that Glenn brings to the table is his strength when working with individuals and organizations in any industry.

Glenn's humorous, insightful speaking style makes him a sought-after keynote speaker and facilitator. He's certified by the New York, Texas, Florida, and South Carolina Bar Associations for delivering Certified Legal Education in the areas of practice management, ethics, and law-firm leadership. He has facilitated strategic-planning sessions with the Orlando Utilities Commission, Valencia Institute, CNL, State Farm Insurance, Comair, and a variety of professional-services firms. His extensive use of stories, history, and philosophy and his understanding of organizational dynamics create an enjoyable learning environment and give him the ability to apply truth from a variety of disciplines.

Glenn graduated with honors from Flagler College in St. Augustine, Florida, with a degree in psychology and philosophy. Following his undergraduate work, he earned his master of divinity degree from Asbury Theological Seminary and a master of arts in organizational psychology from the University of Kentucky. Glenn has been an adjunct instructor for the University of Kentucky in philosophy and for Azusa Pacific University Business School's Leadership Development Program.

He and his wife of twenty-five years, Tami, are the parents of four children. Together they educate their children, attend baseball games, and go to theater performances while taking time to travel as a family. In his personal life, Glenn is dedicated to pursuing a relational connection, spiritual vitality, and professional excellence.

IF YOU'RE A FAN OF THIS BOOK, PLEASE TELL OTHERS

- Write a positive review on www.amazon.com.

- Purchase additional copies to give away as gifts.

- Suggest *Wake-Up Call: The 7 Pivotal Moments That Can Change Everything* to friends.

- Write about *Wake-Up Call* on your blog. Post excerpts to your social media sites such as: Facebook, Twitter, Pinterest, Instagram, etc.

- When you're in a bookstore, ask if they carry the book. The book is available through all major distributors, so any bookstore that does not have it in stock can easily order it.

You can order additional copies of the book from my website as well as in bookstores by going to www.wake-upcallthebook.com. Special bulk quantity discounts are available.

CONSULTING & COACHING ™

Awake Consulting & Coaching can be your non-equity partner that will grow your revenue, increase your profits and make the challenges of leading your business fun! We grow your business by growing the leaders in your business.

We provide the following services to entrepreneurs and executives:

- *Leadership Coaching*
- *Business Consulting*
- *Corporate Training*
- *Event Speaking*

The best place to begin your journey in overcoming mediocrity is with our unique *Executive/Entrepreneur Leadership Profile*. This tool will provide a wealth of information for your ability to lead your business in the future.

- Discover the **Leadership Style** of your entire team
- Understand the **communication preference** of your team
- Diagnose the **current health** of your team and culture
- Develop an **action plan** to move from your current reality toward your desired reality.

There's no need to take one more step alone. Awake Consulting & Coaching can be your non-equity partner in the success of your business. Call us to grow your business by growing your leaders!

1-800-306-8480
www.awakeconsulting.com

Wake-Up Call provides thoughtful insight for the inevitable challenges and choices that every leader must face over the course of a career, and does so with many illustrative real-life examples.

—David Nye, PhD, Engineering Executive

Wake-Up Call is a practical and entertaining blueprint for anyone who wants to do what they do better.

—R. Champ Crocker, JD, Attorney, Cullman, AL

The ancient Greek philosopher Heraclitus once said, "The only constant in life is change." If that's true, our response to change is critical. In *Wake-Up Call*, Glenn Gutek shows leaders how they can make the best of life's inevitable vicissitudes. Mining classic literature, business theory, popular culture, and his extensive experience coaching professionals, Gutek guides readers past potential career landmines and sets them up for genuine success. It's no wonder so many elite leaders already turn to Gutek for guidance. *Wake-Up Call* will enable many more to do the same.

—Drew Dyck, managing editor of Leadership Journal and author of *Yawning at Tigers*

Seven types of wake-up calls—we all experience them. Glenn Gutek provides inspiring examples of awesome leaders from whom everyone can learn, and he writes with excitement in his voice! Gutek shares his unique spin on how we experience insight, success, money, failure, loss, change, and faith, dispelling negative perceptions while instilling a positive mindset.

—Kate Price-Howard, PhD
Go Play, Inc.
Owner and Chief Play Officer
Las Vegas, NV

An amazing story-teller, Glenn's quick wit and profound insights will blow you away.

I wish I had been exposed to all of this stuff early on in my career—it might have spared me some of my most painful lessons learned. Whether a seasoned professional or rookie, you will find your personal "wake-up call" between the covers of this gem of a book.

—Luis Calatayud